# THE ART OF BRIAN COFFEY

BA 1900 **621444** 9334

*Leabharlanna Fhine Gall*
BLANCHARDSTOWN LIBRARY
Inv/01 : 01/BA478 Price IRf13.95
Title: Art Of Brian Coffey
Class: REF 821·914

D1152123

Brian Coffey, *c*. 1930

# THE ART OF
# BRIAN COFFEY

*Dónal Moriarty*

University College Dublin Press
*Preas Choláiste Ollscoile Bhaile Átha Cliath*

First published 2000 by University College Dublin Press,
Newman House, 86 St Stephen's Green, Dublin 2, Ireland

© Dónal Moriarty 2000

ISBN 1 900621 43 6  (hardback)
1 900621 44 4  (paperback)

All rights reserved. No part of this publication may be reproduced,
stored in a retrieval system, or transmitted in any form or by any
means, electronic, photocopying, recording or otherwise
without the prior permission of the publisher.

Cataloguing in Publication data available from the British Library

Typeset in Ireland in 10/12 Sabon and Palatino
by Elaine Shiels, Bantry, Co. Cork
Index by John Loftus
Printed in Ireland by ColourBooks, Dublin

*For Jennifer*

# CONTENTS

# LIST OF
# ILLUSTRATIONS

# ACKNOWLEDGEMENTS

I wish to record my thanks to the following people for their assistance: John Coffey for his kind permission to quote from his father's work and for supplying me with the photographs which feature in this book; Brigid Coffey for her permission to reproduce the illustration she designed for the cover of the special issue of *Irish University Review* dedicated to her father; the staff at the Manuscript Room of Trinity College, Dublin and the library staff in University College Dublin; Marianne Mays for reading an early draft and suggesting improvements; Professor Roger Little for his insights into the art of translation and for his careful reading of chapter 3; Barbara Mennell, Executive Editor at University College Dublin Press, for her enthusiastic support and patience. I am thankful to my parents Kathleen and Patrick for their generosity and encouragement. I would also like to acknowledge the backing of the County Dublin V.E.C. and the support of Mr Séamus McPhillips and Mr John O'Shea, and the rest of my colleagues in St MacDara's Community College

I owe a huge debt of gratitude to my trusted mentor Professor J.C.C. Mays for all his excellent advice, kindness and support. He has guided me towards a deeper understanding of the work of Brian Coffey and of poetry in general.

My greatest debt is to my wonderful wife Jennifer to whom this small book is dedicated. She has allowed me to indulge my fascination for Coffey's work and patiently supported me throughout the past five years. Finally, to my three boys Aidan, Robert and Gareth for reminding me that there is life beyond study and allowing me to commandeer the family computer I say a big thank you.

Dónal Moriarty
*Dublin, December 1999*

# ABBREVIATIONS

The following abbreviations have been adopted and follow quotations in the text:

CD  Stéphane Mallarmé, *Un Coup de dés jamais n'abolira le hasard* in *Oeuvres Complètes*, eds Henri Mondor and G. Jean Aubrey (Paris: Gallimard, 1951)

DH  Brian Coffey, *Death of Hektor* (London: Menard Press, 1982)

DT  *Dice Thrown Never Will Annul Chance*, by Stéphane Mallarmé, trans. Brian Coffey (Dublin: Dolmen, 1965)

PV  Brian Coffey, *Poems and Versions 1929–1990* (Dublin: Dedalus, 1991)

In the Notes and Bibliography:

TCD Trinity College Dublin

# A CHRONOLOGY OF BRIAN COFFEY

| | |
|---|---|
| 1905 | Born (June 8) at Dun Laoghaire, Co. Dublin. His father Denis was the first President of University College Dublin from 1908 to 1940. |
| 1917–19 | Mount St Benedict, Gorey, Co. Wexford. |
| 1919–22 | Clongowes Wood College. |
| 1923–24 | Institution St Vincent, Senlis, Oise. Baccalauréat in Classical Studies. |
| 1924–30 | Completes degree studies in Maths, Physics and Chemistry at University College Dublin (Hons BA, BSc, MSc). Publishes first poems (lost) and represents University College Dublin in boxing. Meets Denis Devlin with whom he shared authorship of *Poems* (1930). |
| 1930–33 | Research studies in Physical Chemistry in Paris under Jean Baptiste Perrin, the winner of the Nobel prize for physics in 1926. Develops an interest in philosophy and meets Thomas MacGreevy. |
| 1933 | (February) *Three Poems* published by Jeanette Monnier in Paris. |
| 1933–36 | At Institut Catholique de Paris, to work with Jacques Maritain. Takes licentiate examination in 1936. |
| 1934 | Meets Samuel Beckett in London. |
| 1934–38 | Contributes reviews to T.S. Eliot's *The Criterion*. |
| 1937 | In Paris to work on his doctoral thesis ('De l'idée d'ordre d'après saint Thomas D'Aquin') |
| 1938 | *Third Person* published at George Reavey's Europa Press. (October) Marries Bridget Rosalind Baynes. |
| 1939 | War breaks out while on holiday in Ireland. Unable to return to Paris. |
| 1939–45 | Spends war years in England teaching in schools. |

1947        Presents doctoral thesis at Institut Catholique; it is accepted.
            Appointed Assistant Professor of Philosophy at St Louis
            University, Missouri.
1948–52     Contributes philosophical reviews and articles to *The Modern
            Schoolman*.
1952        Following a dispute with his Jesuit employers, Coffey resigns
            from St Louis.
1954–69     Teaches sixth–form mathematics in London schools.
1961–65     *Missouri Sequence*, 'Nine-A Musing' and 'Four Poems' pub-
            lished in *University Review*.
1965        Translation of Mallarmé's *Un Coup de dés* published by
            Dolmen.
1967        Edits Devlin's *The Heavenly Foreigner* for Dolmen.
1970–74     Poems in *The Lace Curtain*, nos 3, 4 and 5.
1971        New Writers' Press publish a booklet of poems (*Versheet I*)
            and *Selected Poems*.
1973        Rendering of Neruda's *Twenty Love Poems and The Unhoping
            Song* published in *Irish University Review*.
            Moves to Southampton.
1975        *Irish University Review* (Brian Coffey Special Issue) features
            *Advent*, *Leo* and a comprehensive selection of translations from
            the French of Eluard, Mallarmé and others.
1976        *The Big Laugh*, Sugar Loaf Press, Dublin.
1979        *Death of Hektor*, Circle Press (with engravings by Stanley
            William Hayter).
1982        First trade edition of *Death of Hektor*, Menard Press
1983        BBC radio programme on Brian Coffey (Augustus Young).
1985        RTÉ television programme on Brian Coffey (Seán O Mórdha).
            *Chanterelles, Short Poems 1971–83*, The Melmoth Press, Cork.
1990        *Poems of Mallarmé, Versions in English*, New Writers' Press/
            Menard Press, Dublin and London.
1991        *Poems and Versions: 1929–1990*, Dedalus Press, Dublin.
1995        Dies (14 April) in Southampton.

# 1

# INTRODUCTION:
# SOMATIC SOUNDS
# AND RHYTHMS

'My rhythms are somewhat different from the iambic rhythms that are
common in English, and the sources of my rhythms are very various, partly
French, partly English, partly Irish, partly my own body. Things that move
in my own body are part of my own rhythm.'[1]

Brian Coffey is now acknowledged as a pioneer of Irish modernism and is
closely associated with a small band of writers whose careers began in the
late 1920s and early 1930s. This group included people like Thomas
MacGreevy, Denis Devlin and Samuel Beckett. It is arguable that of all
these writers Coffey is the most misunderstood. He possesses a reputation
as a formidably obscure and cerebral poet, and critics have responded to
the challenge by focusing almost exclusively on the thematic content of
his writing. This, of course, has the effect of hardening into a conviction
the impression that Coffey used poetry as a vehicle for purely intellectual
operations. His poems and translations are undeniably difficult and they
evince great subtlety of thought and feeling. However, I believe that an
alternative approach to Coffey's work – one that engages with the specifics
of his unique poetic mode – will make possible a more informed appreciation of his achievement.

More than any of his contemporaries, Coffey was struck by the fact of
language as sound, and the words that constitute his poems were chosen
for their auditory qualities as well as their meanings. Most poets attend to
the rhythmic properties of words and to the sounds of their vowels and
consonants, but for Coffey the impulse to charge his lines with a kind of
musical tension was unusually strong. The music of his poetry has a
distinctive signature: his lines and stanzas possess a highly reverberant
quality and often while reading through a Coffey poem, we become
increasingly aware of an accumulating store of significant echoes. Coffey
may strike echoes from the previous word or, alternatively, he creates an
unusually live acoustic which enables sounds to echo over pages of

intervening material. I believe that the repetition of sounds and rhythms is the major constitutive principle of his verse. It is a matter of what Beckett called 'fundamental sounds (no joke intended) made as fully as possible'.[2] This book treats of this aspect of Coffey's art and attempts to show how it bears crucially on the meaning of his poems.

Coffey's voice has no analogue, and when I refer to the musical quality of this sound I do not mean that the poems are characterised by the kind of 'harmony' that will appeal to readers who hold fixed opinions about what may, or may not, be pleasing to the ear. In fact, sound patterning is often employed to achieve discord. Coffey loved to experiment with contrasting timbres of sound: clusters of rhymed vowels may often be juxtaposed with others from the opposite end of the tonal scale in order to produce a dissonant effect; a line packed with mouthfuls of nasal consonants may be followed by another with carefully modulated open vowels. Such effects become part of the broad rhythm of the poem; they lend it a dynamic and enrich its meanings.

His rhythms could be unfamiliar, perhaps even alienating, to new readers. The sources of these rhythms are 'very various', as the epigraph makes clear, and it is a fact that Coffey was better able to articulate the rules of French rather than English prosody. He liberated himself from the tyranny of the metrical foot as an organising principle early in his career and opted instead for a line in which stress governed rhythm. His rhythms are instinctive and, without wishing to imply a lack of subtlety, one might even say they have a primal quality.

I believe his conviction that a poet's rhythmic sense was a function of his or her bodily processes is significant. If Coffey's rhythms derive in part from his own body it is equally true that they elicit a physical response in the reader. A reader may experience an enhanced awareness of how the organs of vocal production must work in order to enunciate his carefully sculpted lines and this experience gives rise to an attendant appreciation of the very materiality of words. When we become conscious of this response, and when this response is felt to bear directly on the meaning of the verse, we feel that Coffey has somehow expanded the possibilities of poetic expression.

\*     \*     \*

The remarkable thing about Coffey's distinctive voice is its consistency over a writing career that spanned almost six decades. That his life was marked by some of the major political and cultural upheavals of the century makes his fidelity to the aesthetic values that he established early in his career all the more remarkable.

An appreciation of *Third Person* (1938) is important in this context because by plotting the continuities that link it with later long poems such as *Advent* (1975) and *Death of Hektor* (1979), one can arrive at a more accurate understanding of how Coffey's career developed. As I have argued, the feature that characterises Coffey's best verse, and the one which Beckett described as its most distinguishing quality, is the reverberance of its sound.[3] In this respect, the strange echoic poems that comprise *Third Person* bear a closer affinity to the later long poems than they do to the intervening *Missouri Sequence* (1962), the work for which Coffey is perhaps best known.

It is ironic that the poem that is the least representative of Coffey's style is the one that consistently features in anthologies of modern Irish poetry and has been the subject of most critical attention. Because the present study attempts to respond to the pressing need for discussion of the poet's lesser known work it passes over *Missouri Sequence*. The comparative popularity of the poem has much to do with its accessibility. Written in a conversational mode, its variable lines respond to subjective processes of thought and feeling while registering the exigencies of the outer world. Specific settings of time and place, the particularised descriptions of the environment the poet inhabits, and references to friends, family and the poet's personal circumstances all lend the work a mimetic quality that endears it to many Irish readers.

While the sequence contains eloquent meditations on the pain of enforced exile and the struggle to retain authenticity in a contingent world, the quality of the writing is uneven: the rhymed parable that constitutes the middle section of Part II, for example, is especially slack. *Missouri Sequence* reflects the conditions of its making and this accounts for the sense of strain that one feels reading its final stanzas. Part IV moves towards an unproblematical definition of poetry that sits ill at ease in a work which takes for its subject matter the very real difficulties involved in writing poems and which utilises as a source of creative tension the conflicting demands of 'family cares and crises' and the impulse to write. While the more economic *Third Person* maintains a happy balance between metaphysical insight and existential awareness, *Missouri Sequence* finally settles for a sentimental rehearsal of well worn orthodoxies.

The nature of Coffey's exile must be distinguished from Joyce's, and that of his friends, Thomas MacGreevy, Samuel Beckett and Denis Devlin. It would be wrong to suppose that his move to Paris in 1930 was motivated by a need to escape from an environment that had become increasingly oppressive throughout the 1920s. In fact, it was the wish of Denis Coffey – the first president of University College Dublin and by all accounts an authoritarian in professional and family affairs – that his son further his scientific education. An opportunity to study under Jean Perrin, who had won a Nobel prize in Physics in 1926, was readily seized upon.

Although Coffey and Denis Devlin had been nominated by Beckett as 'without question the most interesting of the youngest generation of Irish poets' we ought not to assume that Coffey shared the antipathy that fuelled Beckett's withering analysis of contemporary Irish poetry in the early 1930s.[4] Indeed, the kind of renunciation implicit in Devlin's remark to Mervyn Wall concerning his decision to join the Diplomatic Corps in 1935 – 'it enables you to get out of Ireland' – is nowhere expressed in any of Coffey's writings.[5] Coffey actually grew to dislike Paris and he returned to Dublin in 1936 hoping to make a living and a home in Ireland. His failure to find employment still rankled several decades later, yet his feeling of personal offence never prompted a generalised condemnation of the Irish Free State.

Unable to return to Paris in 1939 because of the war, Coffey lived with his wife and young family in England until 1947, in which year he was appointed Assistant Professor of Philosophy at St Louis University, Missouri. A principled and sometimes stubborn man, Coffey quarrelled with his Jesuit employers and he resigned his post in 1952. Much to the annoyance of the Jesuits, Coffey refused to leave his university lodgings and his family survived on the charity of a nearby convent and a few neighbours for almost two years. He finally settled in England with his family in 1954 and he taught mathematics in a number of secondary schools until his retirement in 1972.

As *Missouri Sequence* attests, Coffey continued to consider Ireland as his homeland or *patria* during his long exile and he later spoke of it 'as the place where I came from, where I was born and whose airs and earth and so on I have built into my body'.[6] Therefore, if one hears faint echoes of Gaelic rhythms and sounds in his poems, they are there by virtue of his being Irish; they are not self-conscious attempts to incorporate an essential 'Irishness' into his verse. The obvious parallels with Beckett's handling of rhythm and syntax in both his prose and poetry probably owe more to a shared response to French poetry, particularly Eluard's, than to a shared nationality. Indeed, Coffey was more receptive to the complex syntactic operations of Mallarmé, the spiritual lyricism of Claudel and the sur-realist love poetry of Eluard than he was to the heroic example of Yeats.

From what can be inferred from the glancing allusions worked into the later poetry, Coffey's opinion of Yeats was, to say the least, ambivalent. The one short article he wrote about him is important less as a piece of criticism than for the way it interrogates Yeats's sense of an Irish tradition. 'A Note on Rat Island' identifies as folly what nowadays we would call an enabling myth, that is, Yeats's expressed desire to 'preserve that which is living and help our two Irelands, Gaelic Ireland and Anglo-Ireland, so to unite that neither shall lose its pride.' Coffey argues that the origins of 'that which is living' in Irish culture are simply not reducible to two politically and historically opposed groups. Such thinking forgets how 'fruitless paired categories (Gaelic with Anglo-Irish, Protestant with Catholic, . . . etc.) are for thinking social and political reality with, not to mention poetic reality'.[7] Coffey does not cite the grounds of his objections, although it would be fair to assume that one who consistently argued that poetry deals with universals of the human condition would not locate any essence in historically determined accidents. Nonetheless, the article goes on to defend 'The Lake Isle of Inisfree' against Robert Graves's wicked parody of that poem, a parody which suggested that Yeats's early lyric was nonsensical. Arguing from the premise that 'there are poets of sound, or almost . . . [and] there are poets of sense, or almost', Coffey offers different criteria for appraising the worth of the poem. He recognises it as the work of

> a man fascinated by words as sounds, who sought to guide the mobile evanescent qualities of verbal sound . . . into groupings which would exhibit the most richly varied rhythmical quality his language (the English language as used in Ireland) had ever supported until he worked in it.[8]

This is high praise indeed and one suspects that the purely aesthetic standards applied here are the ones by which Coffey would have his own achievement assessed. Yeats is valued for his dedication to the mastery of poetic technique, but what Coffey objected to was the surrounding context of his involvement with the Literary Revival, a movement which he believed was predicated on the assumption that society could be redeemed by enacting the cultural prescriptions of a few and which encouraged a system of patronage that could compromise emerging talents.

By the time Coffey began writing poetry, Yeats had already taken for his subject matter the disparity between the vision in which he so heavily invested, that of a culturally renewed Ireland, and the painful realities of the Civil War, not to mention the increasingly intolerant climate of the recently constituted Free State. He had succeeded in transcending Revivalist thinking by absorbing it into the dialectic of his own poetic development. Dispensing with Cuchulainn and pagan antiquity, Yeats invoked an alternative tradition into which he could inscribe himself, an Anglo-Irish intellectual tradition which included figures like Berkeley, Burke, Grattan and Swift.

Finding and constructing a specifically Irish tradition with which one could identify was felt as an imperative by many poets during the 1920s and 1930s. While Austin Clarke, for example, set the values of

Celtic-Romanesque Ireland against those of the Free State, Padraic Fallon celebrated the peregrinations of the nineteenth-century Irish minstrel, Anthony Raftery. In a disastrous attempt to provide Ireland with a great epic poem on the scale of the *Iliad* or the *Aeneid*, Padraic Colum recounted a Bronze Age saga in the 1,800 line *Story of Lowry Maen* (1937). It would be unfair to suggest that all of these poets were unaware of the disjunction between the idealisations of the Revival and the reality of Irish life in the early decades of the century, yet throughout the 1930s all of them, in their different ways, were implicitly endorsing the values of that movement. According to Patrick Kavanagh, 'the dregs of the old Literary Revival were still stirrable' when he arrived in Dublin in 1939.[9] While he believed the movement was by now discredited, the 'roots in the soil theory' was still in circulation and was heavily sponsored by English publishers who had identified a big market for 'the synthetic Irish thing'. Kavanagh's prompt election as resident peasant poet in the Palace Bar may have raised his local profile but it was a promotion he would later regret.

The pressure to write in a manifestly Irish way was acutely felt by poets in Free State Ireland and the terms in which they had to inscribe their 'Irishness' were now determined by an increasingly powerful ideology of post-colonial state formation which assumed that there was a pure and intact Irish identity 'out there' awaiting full expression. A combination of market forces and the emergence of a bourgeois nationalism, which fed on the representations of Irish identity that these forces demanded were conditions that were hardly conducive to a creative engagement with the very notion of identity itself.

Beckett's analysis of the critical failure of Irish poets to modernise themselves invokes purely literary values and, while he could hardly be expected to conduct an Althusserian analysis of the way the new state apparatuses set about the business of ideological subjection, he intuitively spotted a symptom of it when he identified the disabling effects of the 'entire Celtic drill of extraversion'.[10] By now, Beckett's classification of those poets who were 'aware of the new thing that happened' as distinct from the antiquarians is well known. The antiquarians are castigated for their 'flight from self-awareness'; fixated upon a 'circumference' of stock revivalist themes, they fail to look inward and explore their own subjectivity. Where such an excavation of 'the centre' may take one, Beckett does not say, but the conditions of the undertaking would involve a recognition of the impossibility of unmediated experience and a preparedness to risk alienating oneself for the sake of artistic integrity.

The issues raised in 'Recent Irish Poetry' were undoubtedly the subject of much discussion in the Bar du Depart, where Coffey and Denis Devlin frequently socialised with Beckett when in Paris. While it would be wrong to deduce from Beckett's promotion of Coffey and Devlin that they deferred to his critical opinion, one can safely assume a shared awareness that Irish poets had to liberate themselves from their obsession with the subject of their nationality and attend to what Coffey would later call 'the precious stream or flow of interior life'.[11] By the 1930s the fragmentation of received forms, the rejection of the pretence of the unitary 'I' speaker of lyric poetry and an awareness of the wider European literary tradition had been well established as features of what we now call modernist poetry. In each of their different ways, Beckett, Coffey and Devlin successfully integrated these elements into their writing and produced strikingly independent collections of poetry that have yet to be recognised as important documents in Irish modernism.

Like *Third Person* (1938), Beckett's *Echo's Bones* (1935) and Devlin's *Intercessions* (1937) were published by Reavey's Europa Press and these collections provide a context for Coffey's first collection. Many of the poems in *Echo's Bones* subvert the tradition of lyric poetry by employing the forms of Provençal genres like the *serena* and the *aubade* only to deny the culminating visions that they once featured. The opening section of 'Alba' intimates the promise of some revelatory experience that will attend on the arrival of 'you' – a reference to Dante suggests some association with Beatrice – and then confounds our expectations by suggesting that the arrival of the girl will actually foreclose the possibility of redemption. By way of its title – 'The Vulture'– the opening poem alludes to Goethe's metaphor for artistic creation and implicitly subverts the early Romantic notion of poetic utterance as a restorative process through which man is brought into harmony with himself and nature. Rather than bear witness to a life-affirming mastery of word and thought, writing is now bound up with processes of decomposition and dying. Self-alienation and an acute awareness of the recalcitrance of the materials with which the poet works – 'the unalterable/ whey of words'– are openly acknowledged as conditions of writing.

Not all of the poems are so unremittingly bleak, and flashes of Beckett's dry humour occasionally break through. 'Sanies 1' relates a bicycle journey through north County Dublin and revels in verbal high-jinks that recall Joyce – 'the sycomores are sobbing'– and an early allusion to Chaucer establishes an amusing analogy with the pilgrim's journey to Canterbury. Like 'Alba' and 'The Vulture', 'Sanies 1' obeys the first precept of 'Recent Irish Poetry' by admitting 'the existence of the author'. Having laboured over miles of hilly townland to meet his beloved, the speaker opens up an ironic distance between the experience of seeing her and the act of recording that moment by providing a grammatical analysis of his own writing:

> I see main verb at last
> her whom alone in the accusative
> I have dismounted to love[12]

A preoccupation with Cartesian dualism, often expressed as the disjunction between life and art, and an amoral view of sexual relations that reflects the influence of Schopenhauer – who argued that love is a necessary delusion by which the will to life of the species is enacted – also characterises later poems like 'Cascando' and especially the series of French poems that Beckett wrote between 1937 and 1939. The comparative asceticism of 'elles viennent', which enacts its argument through patterns of variation and repetition, bears a striking resemblance to the distinctive mode of *Third Person*, although it must be added that Coffey's poems testify to an entirely different understanding of the relations between art and life and that they present an alternative, more ethical consideration of the subject of love between the sexes.

Devlin's 'Est Prodest', which strikes the keynote of *Intercessions*, is thematically related to *Third Person* but it develops its argument in a different way. The imagination searches for, but fails to conceive of, an image that will adequately express God's infinite variety. The speaker comments on his own cognitive processes as the thread of imagination is repeatedly broken by the interruptions of reason. 'Est Prodest' proceeds from theological speculation to ethical self-examination and self-exhortation, and concludes by evoking a vision of human society that will reflect His glory. Other poems, like 'Bacchanal', engage with issues that preoccupied English poets, for instance Auden, but make for different, more detached types of commentary than, say, the more politically committed 'Spain 1937'. 'Argument with Justice' could be usefully read against Auden's analysis of Justice in both versions of the verse commentary of *Journey to a War*.[13]

While Coffey and Devlin shared the same religious convictions and brought them to bear on these early works, the inner dynamics of their poems and the voices that articulate them are markedly dissimilar. The fuller reach of Devlin's more extended line permits a continuous stream of intricately related surrealist images and allows for a greater variety of rhetorical devices which lend the poetry an impassioned lyricism, as in 'Est Prodest', or more often suggests an ironic detachment from the persona that speaks the poem, as in 'Entry of Multitudes into an Eternal Mansion':

> Sweetness of blood's vague way across
> The bland white plains of operating tables!
>     I am well in, loose me
>     From these hags these futile
> Visions and discourse and the pomp of signs[14]

Coffey, on the other hand, proceeds by selection and careful placement. The relationship between his short, spare lines and stanzas is more oblique and is determined by a deep impulse to explore and develop aural rather than visual resonances. Tonalities do not respond in a fluid way to the changing feelings of a single speaker; rather, they are framed in the shifting perspectives of the different speakers, all of whom are contained within a single voice. The unique quality of this voice is discussed in chapter 2 and it suffices to mention here that its strangely dislocated and obviously fabricated mode constitutes a more radical admission of the existence of the author than either Devlin's or Beckett's experiments with voice.

Unlike the early work of Objectivist poets such as Louis Zukofsky and George Oppen, these early collections do not constitute the output of a single school despite the shared literary and philosophical interest of their authors. A mutual antipathy to Revivalist prescriptions ought not to blind us to the diversity of their writing. The uncritical coupling of Devlin and Coffey that one often finds in narratives of twentieth-century Irish poetry tends to suggest a similarity of writing without recognising the differentiating features of their respective work.[15] In fact, *Third Person* stands more sharply defined against the backdrop of Irish poetry in the 1930s than either *Intercessions* or *Echo's Bones* and it anticipates subsequent trends in a way that these collections do not. Positive evaluative criteria such as lack of closure, subversive verbal play, textuality, intertextuality, the interpenetration of opposites and, most crucially, an exploration of the relationship between voice and identity, are all displayed in this highly unusual work. It possesses no analogue in Irish writing and those seeking one should turn to a collection like Oppen's *Discrete Series* (1934) which, like *Third Person*, can be read as a challenging response to the high modrnism of Eliot and Yeats. Written in a minimalist mode, both works explore the particular resonances that can be generated when the 'poetry collection' is treated as a literary genre possessed of its own dynamic possibilities.

One cannot advance such claims on behalf of *Third Person* without addressing the question of why Coffey's poetry does not enjoy a much larger readership. His neglect has much to do with the uncompromising nature of the work and its perceived difficulty. Mistaking compression of meaning for gnomic impenetrability, or creative ambiguity for wilful obscurity, many readers flinch from a direct and meaningful engagement with Coffey's work. The following chapters aim to demonstrate that his poems and translations are not the hopelessly obscure texts that some take them to be. Yet Coffey's work is indeed uncompromising in the sense that it never affords the reader false consolation nor does it advance definitive solutions to the problems it investigates. Broad historical processes and the patterns of real life are fully inscribed but so also are the poet's ethical and aesthetic values and the resulting tensions are rarely resolved and integrated comfortably within the structure of the poem. For some readers this constitutes a type of failure on Coffey's part, yet paradoxically, others regard this as the quality that distinguishes his work from the mass of Irish poetry since Yeats.

It could also be argued that the comparative popularity of *Missouri Sequence* and the continued neglect of other worthwhile work are functions of prevailing critical practices. Given the reluctance of practitioners of cultural criticism to engage with matters of literary craft and stylistic technique and their failure to acknowledge the specificities of poetic expression, it is hardly surprising, then, that they cannot accommodate a writer who is simply not exercised by the question of national identity. Coffey's work does not deal with recognisably Irish subject matter nor does it testify to its author's nationality in the way that Irish readers have come to expect. This is why *Third Person* must be considered as a representative work. Like much of Coffey's poetry – his love poems in particular – it explores the universals of the human condition without reference to time or place. It is this non-mimetic and highly experimental quality of his writing that exposes the limits of current critical thinking. The quality that Beckett noted in Jack Yeats's art – 'Strangeness so entire as even to withstand the stock assimilations to holy patrimony, national and other'– is invoked as an ideal and his appreciation of the painter reveals as much about his own ambitions as it does about Yeats's painting.[16] Unassimilable 'strangeness' might also describe the condition of Coffey's poetry. Ironically, despite Beckett's professedly apolitical stance and the dislocated quality that Ireland takes on in his highly refractive imagination, its very presence in his work, indeed his antagonism towards his native country, makes him easier to incorporate within current narratives of Irish writing. There seems to be little room for those who adopted a more truly detached position.

This is not to say that Coffey was indifferent to the cultural and political history of Ireland. Rather, as this study argues, the perspective that Coffey adopts on Ireland is one that has been broadened by learning and lengthened by years of exile. Indeed, the pain of exile is present in *Third Person*, but it is treated as a universal rather than a local experience, and once we begin to understand the collection as a celebration of the power of language to undo fixed structures of opposition and to recognise that it embodies *différance* in a way that was unprecedented in Irish poetry, we begin to realise that its underlying ethos is liberationist in the most profound sense of the word. Its central themes, such as the creative interpenetration of apparent opposites and its advocacy of reciprocal influence, can be extended to include a critique of imperialist ideology.

Indeed the second poem of the collection, 'White', comments on empires and accounts for their inevitable demise in terms that would be endorsed by most post-colonial theorists.

The later long poems, *Advent* and *Death of Hektor*, which are treated in chapter 4, make explicit references to Ireland's political history and her culture, but these references are used to illustrate a much larger argument. There are allusions to Joyce and Yeats yet they are not invoked as representatives or metonyms of a national literature. They are understood as part of a broader tradition that includes Homer, Sophocles, and Mallarmé, and English language poets such as Blake and Eliot. Each of the allusions implies an evaluation of the respective contributions of these writers, and the values that are invoked are moral rather than political or aesthetic. The same can be said about the perspective from which Coffey regards Irish history. His point of view is that of the passivist who is deeply suspicious of all political rhetoric. The reference to the rhetoric of Sinn Féin implies a criticism of the insularity promoted by that movement but this is not to say that Coffey is making the same argument as the revisionist school of Irish historians.

This curiously displaced yet nonetheless broad perspective affords a view of previously unseen and, therefore, unsettling relations. Awkward questions begin to surface and they prompt a different kind of assessment: for example, can we distinguish between the violent nationalism of Sinn Féin and the militant nationalism that precipitated two world wars? To what degree was the success of that movement an effect of political rhetoric? How does the weight of Yeats's achievement compare to that of Homer, who, in Coffey's view, had a greater insight into the human condition and whose works bear witness to a more direct engagement with the world? And by choosing as their exemplars mythological figures who were conquerors, were Yeats and Joyce unconsciously colluding with an ideology that validates the principle of 'might is right' and which underpins the power structures that characterise modern capitalist society. Declan Kiberd's argument that a close reading of *Ulysses* will throw up 'far more evidence of its anti-colonial themes' could very well be true, but the fact remains that Joyce's eponymous hero – however he be tricked up with a passive, modern sensibility in his later incarnation – was the principal architect of what could be justifiably construed as a ruinous imperialist campaign.[17] Coffey's mode is never didactic, but it does challenge readers – particularly Irish readers – to make evaluations that are based on principles other than those invoked by the prevailing and interrelated discourses of politics, history and literary criticism.

To quote pertinent passages from *Advent* and *Death of Hektor* would be pointless here because, once detached, individual lines lose important heights and depths of meaning that are a function of their location within the larger context of the poems. Taken in isolation, the passages that deal with Sinn Féin will read like the posturing of a crank instead of illustrations of a singularly coherent argument. It is not my intention to justify or test the validity of Coffey's opinions on such issues. I want to explore how his later long poems enrich and release meanings through complex patterns of allusion, self-echo and analogy, and to demonstrate how the metrics of these long poems can be understood as developments of formal discoveries made during the composition of *Third Person*.

Chapter 3 deals with Coffey's approach to the act of translation and it occupies a central position in this study for several reasons. Firstly, his work in this area complements rather than constitutes an adjunct to the poetry, and an appreciation of his creative and total engagement with the poetry of Mallarmé and Nerval will enable a greater appreciation of the important dialogue that he conducts with them in the poems discussed in chapter 4. There is another sense in which we can speak of the central position that the translations occupy in Coffey's work. Throughout his career he rendered foreign poetry into English, all the while developing his own understanding of what the task of the translator entailed. Unlike most translators who conform to the dominant Anglo-American model, Coffey sought to preserve the rhythms, syntax and lineation of the original poem, thus signifying its essential foreignness and anticipating *avant la lettre* recent critical thinking about the art.[18] He was not interested in creating the illusion that his translations were not translations but original poems; instead, he preferred to explore the ambiguities and tensions inherent in the original poem and inscribe his own convictions in an obvious way. Coffey plainly did not regard translation as a surrogate for poetry and by rejecting the pretence of the 'the translator's invisibility' – the wholesale adoption of which has assisted in the marginalisation of the art – he staked a claim for translation as a serious and creative literary form possessed of its own integrity.

With the notable exception of J.C.C. Mays, commentators have either ignored Coffey's translations or mistaken the way they reflect the conditions of translation for incompetence or wilful obscurity. The great irony here is that while Irish critics have traditionally acknowledged writers who, like Synge, were imaginative enough to absorb the grammatical constructions and rhythms of Irish into English, they still find it difficult, in an age that celebrates hybridity, to appreciate writers who continue to expand the possibilities of English by opening it up to the influence of other foreign languages. Rather than turn French into English, Coffey turns English into French and makes free use of nonce words, archaisms, literalisms and odd translations that apparently deviate from the sense intended by the author. The resulting texts bristle with meaning and they afford the reader privileged access to complexities of thought and feeling that are peculiar to French poetry.

Coffey's 'versions' have not been published in a single volume – indeed many of them are out of print – and because they demand to be judged under other criteria than those brought to bear on more conventional translations, his exact stature as an Irish translator will be disputed. Two of the works he has rendered into English, Rimbaud's 'Le Bateau ivre' and Nerval's sonnet sequence *Les Chimères*, were also translated by Irish writers. Samuel Beckett's exhilarating 'Drunken Boat' marks a different kind of response to 'Le Bateau ivre' than Coffey's 'The Joy-Mad Ship' and, while both translations have their respective merits, only Coffey's preserves the mystery inherent in the original poem. Derek Mahon's versions of Nerval's sonnets are undoubtedly competent and they will satisfy those for whom elegance and fluency are hallmarks of good translation. Yet, for those who look for something different in translations, elegance and fluency can become specious virtues, especially when the vital grain of the original gets concealed under so much varnish. Coffey, unlike Mahon, refuses to domesticate these powerfully compressed sonnets. By retaining their stylised, medieval quality and working from within the given rhythms and syntax, he conveys the psychological crisis to which they give expression while simultaneously managing to track the dialectical movement that each embodies.

Having compared Coffey's translations with those of Beckett and Mahon, chapter 3 then considers *Dice Thrown Never Will Annul Chance*, Coffey's version of one of the most challenging texts in the whole of French literature and one that anticipates *Finnegans Wake* by several decades, Mallarmé's *Un Coup de dés jamais n'abolira le hasard*. Given the difficulty of the original poem it is not surprising that *Dice Thrown* has been ignored by critics. Despite the incredible demands it makes on the translator, however, it is arguably the finest single translation from the French ever produced by an Irish translator. Coffey loved to translate Mallarmé's poetry and he was eminently qualified for the task. Only a gifted poet, blessed with a command of several languages and steeped in the tradition of Western thought, could render the dense, contrapuntal texture of the poem, convey its essential rhythms and simultaneously inscribe his resistance to its profoundly negative argument.

My discussion of Coffey's method of translation focuses on a small selection of his total output and while comparisons with the work of other translators are made, the chapter involves much close reading and analysis. Given the lack of any previous discussion of these important texts I do not know how else one can do justice to them.[19] Now that the new discipline of translation studies has begun to reappraise the value of alternative models of translation, such as Louis Zukofsky's phonetic rendering of Catullus, perhaps others will be encouraged to undertake a more comprehensive, theory-oriented study of Coffey's contribution.

An earlier passage of this introduction contended that *Third Person* was a progressive collection that foreshadowed subsequent trends in poetry writing. Interestingly there are many parallels between what Coffey was trying to achieve in this work and the thinking of a few forward-looking Irish artists such as Mainie Jellett who, like Coffey, saw her work as a quest for the universal, 'the inner principle and not the outer appearance'.[20] Coffey has consistently argued that poetry must concern itself exclusively with universal truths. Yet, does this mean that Coffey is claiming a privileged status for poetry as a kind of metanarrative that alone among the totality of discourses enjoys an external vantage point on the world? If so, then we feel obliged to conclude that this identifies Coffey as the specific kind of modernist against which most postmodernists define themselves – an experimentalist and an innovator, yes, but one who promotes an aesthetic that is elitist in its quest for autonomy. I would argue that such an understanding of Coffey's art would be mistaken.

Most critics are now prepared to concede that *modernism* and *postmodernism* are contested terms and the particular example of Coffey demonstrates just how difficult it can be to apply them. Those who consider him a modernist might allude, by way of corroboration, to the echoes of Eliot, the evident commitment to matters of design and structure and the deployment of symbolism in *Third Person*. On the other hand, it could be argued that the poems demonstrate an acute awareness of the conditions of language and textuality and are written in a mode that is radically indeterminate, with its shifting pronouns and lack of easily identifiable referents. In the light of these considerations, one could justifiably conclude that the collection anticipates postmodernism by several decades. Coffey's use of Homeric myth in *Death of Hektor* could be understood as a classic modernist strategy until we realise that Coffey is not interested in 'manipulating a continuous parallel between contemporaneity and antiquity' in order to point up an ironic contrast between a heroic past and a diminished present.[21] Rather, *Death of Hektor* interposes itself in the dialogue that Joyce establishes with Homer and destabilises that relationship by contesting the terms in which Joyce understands the *Iliad* and the *Odyssey*.

Coffey's critical intervention amplifies material that is elided in *Ulysses*, but the real focus of his critique is most pertinent here. By way of allusion to *A Portrait*, Coffey implies a tendentious contrast between Stephen's conception of the artist as an impersonal agent whose withdrawal from the praxis of real life is understood as a necessary condition for the creation of pure, self-legislating works of art and the kind of total engagement with the social and natural world evident in Homer's epics. At a touch the argument implicates not only Joyce but a whole continuum of writers including Baudelaire, Mallarmé, Wilde, Yeats and Eliot. The symbolist ideal of the poem as an austere and perfectly ordered field of internal relations uncontaminated by social concerns also permeates the aesthetic of high modernism. Coffey's rejection of this ideal informs much of his critical writing and it is explicitly inscribed into his translation of *Un Coup de dés*, a key symbolist text. While Coffey may share the postmodernist's opposition to poetic autonomy, his objections are based on different grounds. If his poetry unsettles our assumptions, it does not do so with the purpose of subverting bourgeois ideology. Indeed, such a politically committed understanding of the role of the poet would be as objectionable to Coffey as the one promoted by the indifferent modernist.[22] Rather, his highly individualistic aesthetic is underpinned by philosophical principles derived from Aristotle and St Thomas and it is informed by a conviction that the 'making' of poems is determined as much by the physical as by the cerebral processes of the poet, an idea not unlike Charles Olson's notion of the poetic line deriving 'from the breathing of the man who writes, at the moment that he writes'.

While philosophy is an important element of Coffey's poetic, one does not need a degree in the writing of St Thomas Aquinas in order to get anything out of his poems. A preparedness to begin by attending to the sound of the poems – and to the way the organs of vocal production must work to enunciate these sounds – in advance of any comprehension of their conceptual content will take one a lot farther than an intimate knowledge of the *Summa Theologiae*. His work does not demand the type of learning presumed by the author of 'Whoroscope' nor does it require the type of annotation that one finds in scholarly editions of Yeats's poetry. A knowledge of philosophy and a familiarity with French poetry might enrich our appreciation but they certainly will not initiate it.

When it came to philosophy, Coffey was more learned than Beckett or Joyce. Yet he so utterly assimilated the philosophy of Aristotle, Aquinas, Hegel and others into his thinking that their respective influences cannot be proven in the conventional way. Philosophers are not referred to by name; they are rarely invoked by way of quotation and very few passages of his poetry can be adduced as an example of the influence of this or that thinker. Instead of constituting thematic content, it would be more accurate to say that the philosophy informs the perspective from which Coffey regards such themes as love, self-awareness and the relationship between poetry and life.

Alex Davis has examined the way in which Thomistic and Jacques Maritain's neo-Thomistic aesthetics have shaped Coffey's poetic.[23] Davis's argument, however, contains the type of suppressions and misunderstandings that inevitably occur when we project notions about how a particular philosophical influence ought to manifest itself in poetry onto the poetry itself. He is probably correct in identifying the crisis that Coffey underwent in the mid-1930s as an inability to reconcile the conflicting claims of religious faith and poetry, but I would argue that he is mistaken when he suggests that *Missouri Sequence* marks the resolution of this crisis. His essay makes only a passing reference to *Third Person* (thus rendering the subtitle of the book to which it belongs as something of a misnomer) and does not acknowledge the way that collection uses modernist and symbolist strategies to convey its implicit Christian ethos. 'Thirst', for example, which can be understood as an exploration of the state of ignorance that follows on the denial of one's spirituality, works through discontinuity and fracture, and uses symbolist techniques to project an extreme *état d'ame*.

Davis's argument that *Advent* could be partially understood as a reply to Mallarmé's *Un Coup de dés* is incontrovertible. However, when he quotes one or two passages from *Dice Thrown* that supposedly reveal Mallarmé's 'modernist suppositions about language' he is clearly arguing from the questionable premise that the original and the translation are one and the same work. I do not wish to seem pedantic but such an approach blinds him to the fact that Coffey had already inscribed his 'reply' to *Un Coup de dés* into *Dice Thrown*, which makes quoting from that text a decidedly precarious business if one is using it without qualification, as Davis does, to support an argument that involves Mallarmé.

It would be misleading, then, to reduce Coffey's philosophical interests, insofar as they permeate the poetry or translations, to one particular school or tradition. As I hope to demonstrate, the poems incorporate in a highly unusual way, and often at the level of form, the ideas of thinkers like Aristotle, Hegel and other German Idealist philosophers. Such is the allusive and indeed elusive nature of Coffey's poetry that one may hear distantly struck echoes of other writers and thinkers without ever being able to trace them to a specific source. It is possible then, but not probable, that the ethical mode of existence outlined by Kierkegaard in *Either/Or* informs the Existentialist dimension of *Missouri Sequence*. Anyone familiar with the philosophy of Heidegger will be struck by the way those passages of *Advent* that deal with our estrangement from and despoliation of nature resonate with the late essay, *The Question Concerning Technology*. While they may be accidental, such parallels are nonetheless sufficiently striking to warrant the type of extended treatment that lies beyond the ambit of this study.

Aside from the philosophy, there are other aspects of Coffey's output that deserve critical attention. The enigmatic love poems, which explore, among other things, the mysterious interdependence of lack and desire, could be usefully discussed in the light of Lacan's notion of the Other. One suspects that feminist critics will have much to say about how Coffey, as a male poet, constructs male/female subject positions within an economy that depends for its dynamic on unknowable sexual difference. Because other late works like *Leo* (1975) and *The Big Laugh* (1976) depend more heavily for their effect on illustrations and ideograms than the texts discussed here, they call for a different kind of reading. Those with an interest in collaborations between poets and artists will be intrigued by the way Coffey's text interacts with Geoffrey Prowse's surrealist drawings in *Leo*. A truly interesting study might explore the significant and uncanny parallels that link Coffey's early poetry and the later prose fiction of Beckett.

No introduction to Brian Coffey would be complete without some mention of his importance to a group of poets who have operated beyond the boundary of what might be called the dominant poetic tradition in Ireland. The kind of poetry that Coffey wrote could only have been written from the margins. In this respect he cleared the ground for poets like Michael Smith and Trevor Joyce who began their careers in the 1960s and founded New Writers' Press (NWP) out of a sense of frustration at the lack of outlets for experimental poets in Ireland. Coffey's cosmopolitanism – which expressed itself in his reiterated objective to eliminate 'the term irishness [*sic*] from the critical vocabulary' – together with his continued commitment to literary innovation even in the most inauspicious circumstances, and the fact that he was one of the few survivors from the 1930s generation of modernists, distinguished him as an example for these poets. The relationship that developed between Coffey and the founders of NWP was mutually beneficial. He provided them with moral and practical support and he proved to be a valuable contact – with writers like Beckett, for example. In 1971 NWP published *Versheet I*, a small booklet of Coffey's poems, and *Selected Poems*, the first substantial quantity of his work to appear between two covers.

Because his poems and translations tend to foreground the instability of language and interrogate concepts like 'home', 'nation' and identity in novel ways, Coffey appeals to a new wave of experimental Irish poets who are more naturally responsive to Lorine Niedecker and David Antin, say, than they are to Yeats, Kavanagh or Heaney. I refer to poets like Billy Mills, Catherine Walsh and Maurice Scully, whose names do not appear in *The Oxford Companion to Irish Literature* and whose work does not feature in *The Field Day Anthology of Irish Writing*. That they are

Brian Coffey in 1975
*The Irish Times*

excluded in this way is not a matter of concern to these poets who, following the example and the advice of Coffey, have been careful to protect the freedom that their marginalised status has afforded them. Yet it seems a shame that many Irish poetry readers are unaware of Catherine Walsh's very obvious gifts. Her brilliant punning, the way she assembles disjointed, yet perfectly rendered fragments of Dublin argot and her ability to imply simultaneous narratives mark her out from her contemporaries. Billy Mills's inventive and wry reflections on the complex relationship between language and the world will stimulate those who have grown weary of the continued dominance of the unitary lyric 'I' voice in Irish poetry.

Unsurprisingly, the most receptive readers of these *avant garde* poets are British or American. This has also been the case with Brian Coffey and it is hoped that the present study will in some small way correct this anomaly. Each of the following chapters, then, stands independently of the others in the sense that they do not support a single overarching thematic argument. Yet they all proceed from the conviction that the way Coffey's poetry and translations generate and release meaning is still not sufficiently understood. The poems are not the hopelessly obscure texts that some would have us believe they are. In fact there is a great deal of meaning in them, but in order to discover it we must allow the poems to speak to us in their own terms. Coffey's poems are made up out of scrupulously arranged echoes: meanings begin at the point where we begin to hear the way these echoes relate to each other. What I say about the poems also applies to the translations. Their syntax and rhythms catch the vital echoes of the original poem therefore they contain something of its essence.

# 2

# *THIRD PERSON* (1938)

The innocent reader of *The Field Day Anthology* could be excused for supposing that apart from Thomas MacGreevy and Austin Clarke no other poet of the post-Yeats generation had written any worthwhile verse in the 1930s. Terence Brown includes none of the poems from the early collections of Brian Coffey or Denis Devlin in his selection of poetry written between 1930 and 1965. In the case of Brian Coffey these omissions are particularly damaging and they give rise to a mistaken understanding of his development as a poet. *Missouri Sequence* (1962), a pleasing work in its own right yet not in the least representative of Coffey's special sound, now looks set to become his 'Lake Isle of Innisfree'. The frequent inclusion of more accessible passages from it in anthologies of Irish verse reinforce the impression that it marks an emergence into the light after much fruitless experimentation. The truth is not so simple because *Third Person* (1938) is an inventive and accomplished first collection. Any survey of the second wave of Irish modernism that overlooks this work fails to appreciate the full diversity of its subject, because these poems occupy an extreme position at the opposite end of the spectrum to the early efforts of Patrick Kavanagh or Austin Clarke.

*Third Person* marked Coffey's admission to a small band of progressive poets and translators who were published by Europa Press, a concern based in London and run by the cosmopolitan Ulsterman George Reavey. It was coolly received by one contemporary critic who confessed bafflement at an 'idiom . . . of a riddling sort for the understanding of which the reader generally finds himself wanting the key'.[1] This is, in fact, a good description of the initial experience of reading *Third Person*. Yet while the reader puzzles over the lines and stanzas of these poems, their sounds and rhythms are effortlessly absorbed by the memory and reverberate there long after the act of reading has finished.

Paul Valéry, whose theories were an important early influence on Coffey, believed that a poem must stimulate the intellect and keep it in a state of perpetual activity which he designated the 'aesthetic infinite'.[2] Because the intellect controls our other sensations and emotions, poetry excites the whole 'internité'. The reader must never be allowed to feel that he has completely understood the full meaning of the poem, otherwise this sought-after state of activity will be brought to an end. Poems must be difficult but the difficulty must never be too great or the reader will give up; themes must be recognisable so that attention will be attracted and sustained.

A poem like 'Amaranth' deals with experiences and situations familiar to most adults and the language is charged with the rhetoric of recrimination, hurt and threat. Much ingenuity will be expended trying to resolve the apparently random array of pronouns and possessive adjectives into a drama involving two people, yet it becomes increasingly obvious that this is a drama in which a shadowy third person is also intimately involved. Proceeding by a process akin to triangulation the reader tries to establish the exact location of this third person in order to work out how he or she relates to the other two. But this person never seems to occupy a fixed point so that attempts to situate him or her are continually foiled. The enigma has no solution, at least none that I have discovered, but the reader is drawn back, intrigued by the 'aesthetic infinite' that the poem sets in motion. This mysterious situation is later understood in the much wider context of a collection that takes as its central theme the concept of distinction-in-unity, a concept that Coffey ultimately relates to a first cause. I discuss this subject at greater length later in the chapter.

Mallarmé, Reverdy and modernists like Eliot had exploited pronominal confusion but for different ends. The speaking 'I's that populate *The Waste Land* are really secondary voices regarded from the outside by Tiresias, their respective registers and styles being themselves demonstrations of the various themes of the poem. On the other hand, the voice of *Third Person* is really a third term capable of simultaneously apprehending contrasting perspectives on a single moment or situation. The speaker is removed from, yet paradoxically involved in, the implied drama, an effect that anticipates the kind of ontological indeterminacy that has become a feature of recent fiction, for instance John Fowles's *Mantissa* or John Banville's *Ghosts*, where the narrator takes on an eerie insubstantiality as he moves fluidly between states of physical being and ghostly non-being, much like the speaker in 'I Can Not See With My Eyes'. In this poem a situation is described from the perspective of a third-person speaker whom we assume to be dramatically absent. The conclusion of the poem delivers a surprise, for it is only there that we learn that the situation implicates this speaker in a significant way.

'Amaranth' seems to veer between dramatic monologue and antiphon. A silent auditor is initially implied yet as the poem unfolds we sense that somewhere in its course the roles have been reversed. This impression is created by a movement into regular stanzas which seem to respond to each other in the manner of an antiphon. While the distinct patterns and styles of the voices heard in *The Waste Land* suggest the separate identities of the speakers, all of Coffey's poems are delivered by a single voice which maintains the same register despite the apparently random shuttling between singular and plural forms of first-person pronouns.

The voice is elevated, at times it has a chanting quality and it is characterised by a pedantic refusal to contract groups of words. These poems are devoid of regionalisms; there is nothing in the poems to suggest that they came from the pen of an Irishman. The repeated use of the form 'shall', which had been dropped from the vocabulary of almost every Irish poet after Synge, together with the frequent employment of syntactic parallelism and heavily stressed monosyllables, give the verse a faintly Biblical quality. Add to all this a compulsion to explore the permutations available within fixed sets of words and one hears a voice that anticipates the narrative style that Beckett began to evolve a decade later in *Texts for Nothing*:

> Where would I go, if I could go, who would I be, if I could be,
> what would I say, if I had a voice, who says this, saying it's me?[3]

The poems are lyrically reponsive in that they plot, yet do not move smoothly through, an emotional curve. There is a sense in which the speaker is distanced, possessed with enough coherence to bend thought and feeling into the structures of his own highly patterned and formal language.[4] Social contexts and recognisable emotions are evoked but the lines do not flow smoothly in the manner we have come to associate with the lyric, their stylised quality creating the kind of detachment characteristic of Beckett's plays. This detachment has the effect of holding narrative content at a remove and it provides Coffey with the space in which he can conduct his verbal and philosophical researches into the enigma of human relationships. In an early letter to Thomas MacGreevy, Coffey expressed a preference for poems that were 'addressed to the intelligence rather than the affectivity'.[5]

Part of Coffey's project in *Third Person* was to reveal as mysterious that which is taken for granted and for Coffey one of the fundamental mysteries was 'why one person loves another'.[6] The poems do not try to clarify or dispel and there is no attempt to analyse in psychological terms why love can easily pass into animosity or why desire is continually frustrated. The drama of division is simply enacted through changing pronouns and possessive adjectives: 'we' splits into 'I' and 'you', 'ours' divides into 'yours' and 'mine'. Occasions of separation and discord are sprung upon the reader without any explanation beyond the obvious: 'By glens of exile/ if she turns/ love was needed' (*PV* 36).[7]

The essence of what it is to be human depends on such things remaining mysteries and it is from their frank acknowledgement of the contingency of human life that these poems draw their life. Coffey, in his interview with Parkman Howe, discusses this subject: 'Now there is a zone of darkness in us which we can't get into focus. One isn't in the position of having oneself in focus.'[8] Presumably Coffey would argue that dislocation and aporia are not exclusive to modern life but are ontological givens of the human condition. *Third Person* plainly shows that it is a universal and timeless truth that people will always be attracted to others, form relationships and subsequently sever or endanger them for reasons they do not fully understand.

The singular lack of specific reference to times and places and the conspicuous absence of the furniture of twentieth-century life are part of an attempt to strip away all accident in order to lay bare such universals. It is always dangerous to assume that the values a poet admires in the work of others are necessarily borne out in their own poetry, but some of Coffey's critical writing does bear on *Third Person*. Coffey praised Denis Devlin's ability to work 'at the level of things deindividualised without having become abstractions'. The distinction is important: the people in *Third Person* are not stock figures nor are they archetypes. Coffey liked 'Bacchanal' because its figures were 'realised in all times and all places'. Devlin's treatment of the theme of revolution was preferred to Auden's because the latter's historical allusions implicated his poetry in 'mere topicality, here today and gone tomorrow'.[9]

Yet real places do impinge on Devlin's poetic consciousness, albeit only to serve as springboards from which to launch flights of the imagination, like the railway station in 'Daphne Stillorgan' or the eponymous Liffey Bridge. The exclusion of proper nouns from the severely restricted vocabulary of *Third Person* distinguishes it from the work of Coffey's contemporaries. Anything so specific as the geographical allusions in Beckett's 'Sanies I', or, for that matter, so specifically modern as the act of cycling, would have a localising effect on a work that seeks to identify and explore experiences that are as perennial and universal as the activities to which it alludes: giving, taking, tending fields, leavetaking, fishing, sailing and needlework.

A lack of firm sense of location and physical space lends the poems a two-dimensional quality that leaves the reader undecided as to whether these references are literal or figurative. The employment of archaism ('the thimble barque') and metonymy ('white sails') to denote the vessel in which voyages are to be made certainly has the effect of raising doubts about its materiality (*PV* 26, 33). So many poems like 'A Drop of Fire' and 'Patience No Memory' seem to end by recording rupture and separation but the reader is never quite sure whether the figures are physically proximate while metaphorically and emotionally distanced, or if a physical space actually separates the two. This blurring of the distinction between the figurative and the literal creates an imaginative zone in which the laws of space are suspended and it calls to mind the poetry of Paul Eluard one of whose lyrics, 'Le front aux vitres . . .' ends with the beautiful lines: 'Et je ne sais plus tant je t'aime/ Lequel de nous deux est absent.'[10]

Coffey's treatment of time is similar to his treatment of space. In an attempt to convey emotions and states of mind that are constant and which cut across differences of time, he suspends any sense of temporal progression. A striking feature is the frequency with which so many poems open with simple declarative utterances which are constructed with the verb 'to be': 'This is not done for sport' (*PV* 26), 'The stars are standing in the sky' (*PV* 29) and 'Tired trees above water / are your eyes' (*PV* 30). The present tense is maintained with the result that the successive units out of which the poems are constructed seem to float in time rather than mark an advance through it.

'Thirst' is typical in this respect. It opens with a series of images that seem loosely related by an association with water and the natural world, yet no vital link seems to connect them to each other or to the title (*PV* 31). The long central section seems sharply discontinuous with what precedes it but its presentation of an extreme state of alienation and solipsism reflects backwards. The reader recovers the meanings latent in these opening images which are seen in retrospect as projections of an extreme '*état d'âme*'. Other important links are submerged in the colour symbolism which conveys the theological burden of the poem. In Christian art, green has traditionally stood for hope and the significance of the 'green stone' lying motionless on the sea floor as a symbol of the renunciation of hope is amplified later. Anaphora and syntactic parallelism accelerate the rhythm of the central passage and the vertical stacking of the lines intensifies and continues the sense of downward motion initiated by the image of the sinking reed.

> He has desired not to desire
> he has hoped not to hope
> he has no part where he is
> he will have no part where she is
> he is white in the frozen fire[11]
>
> (*PV* 31)

Because he relies on the power of symbol and on the associative properties of his elemental imagery, Coffey is not dependent on narrative to lend cohesion to the units and fragments that comprise his poem.

'Thirst' is about the state of ignorance that necessarily ensues when a person denies his spirituality and permits himself to be governed by irrational passions. It contributes to the implicit Christian ethos of *Third Person*. Anyone even vaguely familiar with the writings of St Thomas will understand the relationship between epistemology and ethics posited by these lines, the first three of which could be read as a series of rhetorical questions, as if the speaker were struck by the absurdity of 'his' predicament.

> Never best but the whore's caress
> never to be understood
> never to understand
> Want and surfeit
> fire

By abandoning himself to exclusively carnal pleasures 'he' mistakes the lesser for the greater good and therefore exists in a contradictory state of lack and excess.

Fichte argued that if man is to be in harmony with himself he must belong in a community with others. The extreme state of alienation described in 'Thirst' – 'lost to self her me' – is projected into the symbol of fire. Existing alone it is removed from an environment in which it can interact with the other elements. For Coffey, the creative interaction of opposite elements signified an ideal union and the motif possibly reflects his Surrealist influences. A remembered moment of fulfilment in 'A Drop of Fire' is figured as a synthesis of opposites: 'Where fountains danced once in the sun/ the owl takes his evening flight' (*PV* 29).[12] Fire and water are blended harmoniously while the fountain itself embraces the upward and downward motion of the water. Whether the separate elements possessed a symbolic significance for Coffey seems to be a point worth considering. Poems consistently identify the male principle with images associated with fire while others, like 'Gentle' and 'Spurred', identify the female with images of water.

While it requires the reader to make the kind of adjustments that so many modernist poems demand, 'Thirst' does not document an exclusively modern experience, despite the final echoes of Archibald MacLeish's 'The End of the World'.[13] Allusions to Eliot subsist like watermarks in the text and I want to return to these later, but for now it suffices to remark that Coffey's poetry is complex for precisely the opposite reasons that the early poetry of Eliot was complex. *Third Person* is difficult not because it self-consciously attempts to reflect the complexities of an age that had renounced the traditional claim that poetry could impart a universal truth. It is difficult because the truths that Coffey tries to unveil are inherently complex.

In abstract terms *Third Person* can be best understood as an extended probing of the paradox of union based on difference, a paradox that marks every meaningful human relationship. This was a theme that endlessly fascinated Coffey and a later poem, 'Answering Mindful', spells it out in very explicit terms: 'Do not doubt deep the difference/ lacking which two make no one' (*PV* 198). Coffey's position on this issue contrasts sharply with that of Eluard whom he highly regarded. For Eluard, love in its ideal form involved utter absorption of one in the other. In its most exalted state love could be expressed in terms of absolute knowledge of the other: 'On ne peut te connaître/ Mieux que je te connais'.[14] 'The Enemy', one of the later poems in *Third Person*, flatly denies such epistemological possibilities.

In his later poetry Coffey would deal with this theme of distinction-in-unity in more discursive and expanded forms, but what marks *Third Person* out as such an impressive achievement is the way it realises its conceptual elements through form. Its closest contemporary analogue is arguably Beckett's *Murphy*, which Coffey had read in manuscript as early as 1936. *Murphy* is a work that ought to be read against *Third Person*; at times, indeed, it seems as if the two works are parts of an ongoing dialogue. Both examine and ultimately refute the possibilities of Cartesian dualism for example, and one wonders whether the futile and comical attempts of Beckett's eponymous hero to attain to a 'matrix of surds' were on Coffey's mind when he penned the final lines of 'Thirst': 'it is so difficult/ to be nothing at all' (*PV* 31).

The key to unlocking the latent conceptual content of *Third Person* is to be found in the peculiar way it brings words into relation with each other: polysemy, omitted punctuation, deviant syntax, tautology and paradox can be listed among the many devices employed. The opening poem, 'Dedication', provides a good example of this:

> For whom on whom then
> and before
> whose eyes desired turned

> (*PV* 23)

The final line of this first stanza can be understood in a variety of ways depending upon whether the reader chooses to understand 'eyes' as the subject of the verb, or whether 'desired' is in fact an adjective, in which case 'eyes' are objects of desire. Other meanings are activated when the reader speculates on the direction of the turning. These eyes could be turning towards the speaker or turning away from him in which case the presence of a third person is implied. The Metaphysical conceit of eyes as both organs and objects of perception is maintained throughout the poem and is of course relevant to a central theme of *Third Person* – namely, the resolution of opposites into a third, higher term.

The final stanza recapitulates this theme by using parallelism and antithesis in a clever interplay between sameness and difference:

> For whom pain is not loss
> For whom loss of is not pain
> For whom want of is pain of loss

Difference is asserted between two words commonly regarded as similar in meaning. The second line, by way of transposition, says the same thing but in a different way. Aristotelian logic then gives way to Hegelian logic in which these two 'antithetical' states are sublated into a higher state of 'want'.

'White', in many respects the ethical keynote of *Third Person*, develops the concepts implicit in 'Dedication' and extends them into the arena of human activity. The poem implies an ideal model of human growth and development yet acknowledges the realities of history. More than all this it celebrates with great wit and audacity the ability of language to transcend rigid structures of thought.

> They do not move as we do
> given they gave taking above
> they see they are not seen
>
> No number we may number
> climbing each term other
> empire to empire not the same
>
> Love opens light to light
> love takes light from light
> love closed light lives in light
>
> No shadow in the white shadow
> flame and gift and
> sails rise on wind
>
> Think no flower no surface
> no smile no extreme star
> think you can see no soul
>
> (PV 24)

Built out of two antithetical units which interact to make up a third term, the opening line embodies with great compression the central theme. The next line accords with this constitutive principle but in a different way. The verb 'to give' has many meanings including 'to value (something) at', the sense in which it is used here. But the unusual juxtaposition 'gave taking' again shows Coffey enacting the theme at the level of form by bringing into relation terms that seem flatly opposed. By punning on the verb 'to see' Coffey again connects two antithetical statements. The next stanza with its advocacy of dialectical growth ('climbing each term other') has discernible traces of German Idealist philosophy. Fichte's revolutionary thesis that the self could only develop through its recognition by others and of others in human society, seems especially relevant to the arguments of 'White' and 'Thirst', as does the following quote from a lecture he delivered in 1794: 'The social drive aims at *interaction*, *reciprocal* influence, *mutual* give and take, *mutual* passivity and activity.'[15]

Hegel developed this idea into his famous analysis of the master and slave and went on to warn of disastrous consequences if society did not check the unfettered pursuit of private self-interest. A dialectical model of expansion based on an economy of giving and taking must have seemed like a remote ideal in a decade that witnessed the burgeoning of Fascism in Europe and when Charles de Gaulle could write: 'The perfection preached in the Gospels never yet built up an empire.' 'White' concedes the point. Empires are recurring historical phenomena yet each one is destined to crumble because it cannot develop dialectically: empires by definition are built solely upon taking.

The epiphanic central stanza of 'White' defines love in terms of light, a symbol which, besides having a unifying function in *Third Person*, firmly establishes its Christian ethos. By stressing the interdependence of perception and thinking, the soul and the physical world, the final stanza amounts to a rejection of Cartesian dualism. The Aristotelian and Thomist in Coffey could not accept that knowledge and awareness of oneself presupposed sense-perception. This closing stanza contains another remarkable effect that possibly reflects the influence of Mallarmé. The imperative 'think' and the repeated negatives confront the reader with the task of imagining the absence of something that is manifestly present in the text, a task which, in the words of Karl Heinz Stierle, involves 'transcending the difference between position and negative counter-position.'[16]

The title of the poem may seem curiously at odds with its argument which affirms the interdependence of opposites and where all is not black and white. But it can be brought into relation with the poem if we are prepared to accept that there is a certain irony involved in evoking the colour white through the medium of black print. If 'White' were to be printed on a black page it could feasibly be entitled 'Black'.

Poems that foreground this theme of related opposites and that are primarily conceptual in content are markedly regular in form. 'White' and 'One Way', important points of reference in *Third Person*, possess their own symmetry. 'One Way', the last poem (*PV* 38), is built out of repeated units that seem to reduce geometrically.

> Given what he has not given
> he sees what he has not seen
>
> Taking what he has not taken
> he hears what he has not heard
>
> No worst fear
> no best light
> constraint constrained
> to work himself out
>
> he breasts tide's breast

The second stanza iterates exactly the syntactic structure of the first. The process of reduction accelerates in the next stanza: the grammatical structure of its first two lines is identical while the third extends the principle to the point where it can proceed no further. The employment of polyptoton (the repetition of words by varying their word class) skilfully enacts the sense of 'constraint'. The concluding lines signal a passage from solipsism to realisation and finally to engagement with the outer world. Parkman Howe argues that Coffey's claim that 'One Way' comments on Samuel Beckett's life does not 'further clarify the poem or Beckett's character'.[17] However, James Knowlson's record of Beckett's treatment and subsequent return to health from a syndrome of physical and pyschological illnesses, under the therapist Dr Bion, does provide an interesting gloss to the poem.[18]

The outer poems of *Third Person* have been discussed in some detail because within their highly compressed and carefully balanced forms they define an ideal and philosophically sanctioned code which stresses the value of reciprocal exchange in all social groupings. Implicit in the symbol of light is the suggestion that such a code has also been theologically ordained. An ideal relationship is a union predicated on difference, but the bulk of *Third Person* demonstrates that negotiating this difference can be an extremely difficult task, one that requires patience and skill.

While the collection does imply an idealised model of perfect reciprocity it also acknowledges that sexual relations are marked by a strong undertow of enmity. This latent enmity is the price of necessary difference. 'The Enemy' probes this paradox through myth and allusion. It is spoken by a 'we' voice, a notional grouping of women who speak out of their common yet individual experiences, hence the shuttling between 'he' and 'they. 'We' are closely identified with a female figure who is the mythical embodiment of the essential feminine principle, the principle that differentiates these notional groups:

> What they did if she smiled
> 'let her alone we can wait'
> we can not do
> burning as she
> to a different end
>
> (PV 32)

Despite this close identification, a necessary distance separates the speaker(s) from this protean figure and the ambivalence of her elusory nature is nicely conveyed in the second stanza: 'If she would condescend only/ tranquil fields silence on earth'. This is an unrealisable wish and the enjambed sense of 'only' suggests that a moonlike 'silence on earth' is too high a price to pay for her assent, as this would necessarily entail an end to difference. 'We' are thus held in tension between the oppositional pulls of 'she' and 'they'.

While 'The Enemy' attempts to examine this difference by way of allusion and myth, other poems demonstrate how it expresses itself in the world of social relations. Most of these poems focus on a couple, theoretically the embryonic form of an ideal society. Yet free will, passion and chance, in short, the very things that define the 'human condition', continually threaten to sunder these relationships. The palpable tension that one feels reading *Third Person* is generated by this conflict between the ideal and the reality.

Repetition plays an important role in maintaining this tension. The recurring leitmotif of giving and taking which is bound up with the symbol of light, evokes the ethical imperatives implicit in 'White' and functions as a metonym for the perfect reciprocity upon which all relationships and unions must be grounded. As the poems demonstrate, however, a perfect system of giving and taking is incredibly difficult to maintain. The conditions of its success include a willingness to accept what is given and a preparedness to wait patiently for it. Conversely the whole system also depends upon a willingness to give and to attend patiently to the other in order to discover what it is that the other needs. This, in turn, depends on a willingness to communicate. The unexplained refusal of the woman in 'Gentle' to disclose 'the charm of secret' frustrates the man's search for 'the form of touch she needs' (PV 34). Coffey's analysis of this delicate circuit of exchange infers the necessity of a much larger complex of virtues that includes patience, charity, temperance, hope, fortitude and forgiveness.

Many of the poems in *Third Person* strike a fine balance between metaphysical insight and existential awareness, sometimes ironically conveying both perspectives at the same time. A great deal of wit and sophistication is displayed and reading these poems one is reminded of the 'alliance of levity and seriousness' that T.S. Eliot noted in the seventeenth-century English Metaphysical poets. The conclusion of 'All We Have' is deeply ambiguous. Through clever exploitation of the line break, Coffey makes two meanings available: it can be read as an unforgiving refusal to give, or, through its obvious association with 'White', it could be understood as a rational statement of the terms which ought to govern a relationship – as in, 'take only what is given'. 'Content' similarly uses the line break to play on both senses of 'just':

> There is time just
> if you can see
> to make an act of love
>          *(PV 28)*

Seeing, which has spiritual and epistemological significance in scripture and Thomistic philosophy, assumes a central importance in a work whose key symbol is that of light, the Aristotelian medium of sight. Love is predicated on an ability to see and be seen. However, the arrangement of words – 'just/ if you can see' – also suggests the difficulty of maintaining mutual visibility in a transient world and reflects, as it were, the existential conditions on the ground.

The titles of some of the poems encapsulate this dual perspective. 'Patience No Memory' echoes a passage that defines 'here' as a place where the eponymous virtue is lacking: 'never is nothing here/. . . ./ patience the lost word unsaid' *(PV 33)*. Alternatively, it could be read as an injunction – 'be patient and forget'– addressed to the woman and delivered from an objective vantage point.

Difficulties usually arise when individual wills do not converge. The opening stanza of 'Amaranth' describes a situation in which the preoccupation of someone silently observed is set against the pent-up desire of the speaker: 'Your needles framed a lilac quilt/ there was patience in my need' *(PV 25)*. The respective positions of the echoing phrases 'Your needles' and 'my need' give added point to this divergence of separate wills. No allegorist, Coffey describes a world where often the only reward of virtue is virtue. A gratifying response may not accrue to one who displays 'patience in helpless need', as this poem and 'Third Person' suggest.

A source of much mystery has to do with the way Coffey continually implies a prior hurt, one that has been inflicted outside the temporal frame of the poem. There are no narrative preliminaries. We are never told why the woman in 'Gentle' 'lives in pure loss alone' (*PV* 34) or why the man in 'I Can Not See With My Eyes' sets out in his 'thimble barque' (*PV* 26). The principle of cause and effect is simply acknowledged. Yet while the cause is never clearly identified, the known emotional effect provides the dynamic of the poem thereby becoming a cause in itself. Many of the poems, then, begin *in medias res*.

'Patience No Memory' illustrates the point well. It begins with a separation brought about by a lack of patience, a virtue which can anchor relationships and one which had a special significance for Coffey. The dynamic is provided by the distinctive *Third Person* voice whose movement between different perspectives gives the poem its modulating tonalities. The pressure behind the initial address conveys the intensity of an emotion experienced at first hand while the echo of 'Women Kind . . .' establishes a context of shared experience. The voice abruptly switches to that of a third person commentator which frankly identifies the crux of the poem: 'He turns to life/ she gives light to love' (*PV* 33). It moves on to sketch briefly a series of stylised landscapes, which are really projections of negative and positive spiritual states, before finally doubling back into direct address, except that this time the auditor is the initial speaker and the mood is unambiguously imperative.

The trajectory of the poem can be traced through its shifting tonalities: anger, frank detachment, reasoned persuasion and, finally, urgent address. Individual stanzas and discrete capitalised groupings within stanzas frame these different tonalities, as they do in all the poems. By initially suffusing Christian symbols with negative meanings – 'dawn charged with wet roses/ red as anger/ white as pain' – Coffey registers the power of intense emotion. The reappearance of these symbols in a more positive context holds out the possibility of recovery, however.[19] The theme of the poem is disarmingly simple: life must go on and the pain and anguish that follow on separation cannot be indulged for too long. 'She', like 'he', must 'turn to life' rather than allow herself be 'turned to stone'. But what makes the poem remarkable is the way it blends detachment and engagement, distance and immediacy, feeling and thought.

I have discussed how the repetition of motifs and symbols throughout *Third Person* invokes moral imperatives, provides additional contexts for individual poems and unifies these poems into a coherent whole. Repetition of consonantal and vocalic sounds occurs at a more local level and it is often the constitutive principle of whole lines and stanzas. Coffey once wrote that 'words demand consideration in those of their properties which are not matters of sense and meaning but, instead, affairs of sound and sensuality'.[20] One of the effects of reading *Third Person* is a new awareness of sound as the primordial matter of language. The way

Coffey uses repetition to organise his sounds into dense clusters deflects attention from what is being signified to the actual process of signification itself. In his discussion of the role of repetition in the work of Beckett, Steven Connor notes:

> It is repetition more than any other trope which draws the attention of the reader to the medium of language. . . . It is at the moment when we recognize that a repetition has taken place that language begins to bulk in our apprehension as arbitrary, systematic and material.[21]

This describes the experience of reading the last line of 'Thirst'. By the time one has reached the fifth 'nothing' the word has almost become a sound drained of any meaning – an effect which paradoxically enacts the meaning of the word.

Lines like this are easily remembered but such is Coffey's gift for creating cohesive patterns of similar sounds that whole stanzas are often absorbed into the memory long before their content is understood. This has much to do with the way a word seems to evolve out of the one before it. In 'Amaranth' we have the following phonetically linked pairs: 'lilac quilt', 'patience in', 'broken on', 'sand and', 'they say' and 'broken in' (PV 25). Sometimes a particular syllable will be sounded in every word of a line: 'For better or for worse' (PV 28). Polyptoton and ploce (the repetition of words without intervening words) are combined in this startling paradox: 'All get what all want/ wanted wanted in vain' (PV 26).

Whole stanzas are often composed out of a few repeated sounds so that they each seem to possess their own particular acoustic. Most of the fifteen words that constitute the second stanza of 'White' contain sounds that reverberate in the nasal cavity, creating a dark tonal quality. Lines threaten to thicken and clot at any moment because of the muscular gymnastics required for the articulation of their many stopped consonants. The poem advances through contrasting tonalities. The bright vowels, liquid consonants and comparatively fewer stops of the next stanza have the effect of opening up the sound again.

Coffey often echoes the expressive sound qualities of related words to connect them and reinforce their meanings. The sense of these lines is enhanced by the heavily stressed and alliterated k's: 'He as we find him/ makes each black wreck more clear' (PV 27). The drastic moment of separation and uprootedness featured in the fourth stanza of 'Spurred' derives much of its dramatic force from the alliterated ch sound of the stressed verbs, 'wrenched', 'chokes' and 'clutch'. Anaphora, a figure of repetition in which the same word is repeated in successive lines or clauses, augments the effect. Movement becomes a matter of urgency in the concluding stanza and the rhymed imperatives 'Race' and 'chase' reflect the sense of the title (PV 30).

Internal rhyme is a key device in *Third Person* but Coffey does not employ it to sound 'the Irish note'– to borrow Seamus Heaney's phrase.[22] Austin Clarke, who apparently disliked the collection, must have missed the intricate sound patterning in the concluding stanza of 'The Enemy' in which every syllable is phonetically linked with at least one other.[23] The interlacing of words from Dante's *Purgatorio* into the texture is remarkable – the chiming of 'ocean' and '*Io son*' is, of course, thematically relevant (*PV* 32).

Lines acquire a deeper significance when they echo distinctive sounds from a previous poem. The way Coffey uses contrasting tempos and tonalities to create the conditions in which echoes can be sounded over such a distance merits some attention. 'A Drop of Fire' which precedes 'Spurred' concludes on a moment of violent separation and energetic movement:

> The hand you use to break from me
> forces you closer to the thorn
> while I burn along the blood
> while I rage and rend the bone
>
> (*PV* 29)

The emphatic iambs and the heavily alliterated *b* and *r* sounds contrast sharply with with the suspended rhythms and long vowels that open 'Spurred'. Note how these effects interact with the context suggested by the previous poem to create a sense of spent energy.

> Tired trees above water
> are your eyes
>
> Does the water-lily think
> such lights amaze
> Silvers by reeds
> detain the dragon-fly
>
> (*PV* 30)

All time and movement is suspended in these discrete circuits of mirroring in which each image seems to be entranced by its own image reflected on the surface of the water. By repeating the motif each successive circuit in a way reflects the others.[24] The mood of repose that attends such moments of self-reflection is briefly established until the outside world breaks in: 'All this is wrenched from roots/. . .'. Rilke's *Requiem* laments the fragility of such moments of perfect mirroring: 'Laß uns zusammen klagen, daß dich einer/ aus deinem Spiegel nahm.'[25] The heavily stressed and repeated *r* sounds and the return to the iambic beat recall the last line of 'A Drop of Fire' powerfully conveying the inevitability of rupture and the circularity of pleasure and pain.

By restricting himself to a vocabulary of words that rarely exceed two syllables, and by careful placement of stress, Coffey creates an environment in which vowels resonate with a clarity that is rare in Irish poetry.[26] A visual analogue of this aspect of Coffey's sound is Piet Mondrian's use of clearly defined primary colours, his vertical and horizontal lines framing them much like Coffey's consonants do his vowels. In 'Les Mots Anglais', Mallarmé wrote that vowels were the flesh of the word beneath which lay the framework or skeleton of consonants.[27] The same essay attempted to analyse the symbolic significances of letters and sounds. The appendix on p. 119 selects some sounds and suggests their possible significance in the context of *Third Person*.

In an article entitled 'Assonance and Modern Irish Poetry' J. Patrick Byrne, a contemporary critic, praised Austin Clarke's use of 'the more delicate instrument of assonance'. Clarke's vowels, he wrote, 'sound gently but persistently till they permeate the whole'.[28] F.R. Higgins, whom Beckett had famously categorised as an 'antiquarian' along with Clarke and others, is also cited as an exemplar of what was considered to be a distinctively Irish way of using vocalic sounds in modern poetry. Higgins, Byrne argued, uses internal assonance on identical or closely related vowels to 'keep the atmosphere proper to the poem'. He cites the following passage from 'The Inn of the Dead Men' to illustrate his point:

> Here even, my dearest, earth trembles in stillness;
> And between hill and weir and the green breadth of mearings
> Lean death makes a clearing, . . .[29]

Verse like this, I suggest, accords more with traditional notions of euphony with its falling cadences and smooth modulations from and returns to a tonic vowel.[30]

Coffey's verse is, to maintain the analogy with music, positively atonal: dissonant intervals of sound are explored in a manner more reminiscent of Schoenberg than Schubert. Closed and open vowels are often juxtaposed in pairs which are then subsequently reversed: 'floating reed'/'green stone' (*PV* 31) or 'green blade'/ 'a lake a tree' (*PV* 25). Stark vocalic contrasts can often give point to direct opposites: 'From the womb/ to the grave. . .' (*PV* 28). In this example, vowels reinforce the separatedness rather than the fusion of elements: 'dark the root of the flame' (*PV* 25). Coffey will often run through a whole range of these sounds over a short distance: 'Those you clutch at/ are eyes you dare not see (*PV* 30). In this respect interesting comparisons can be made with contemporary poets that Coffey probably never heard of at the time, such as the English Objectivist Basil Bunting whose verse abounds in similar acoustic devices:

Weeping oaks grieve, chestnuts raise
mournful candles.

(First Book of Odes)

Since I have trodden Hino mountain
noon has beaten through the awning
over my bamboo balcony, evening
shone on Amida.[31]

(Chomei at Toyama)

Alternatively, vowels from one end of the vocalic scale reverberate with enough insistence to constitute a ground over which others from the opposite end are intoned to create a texture of widely spaced sounds. The long, dark vowels of the repeated relative pronouns 'whom' and 'whose' in 'Dedication' function rather like pedal points over which the brighter sounds in stressed words like 'eyes' and 'pain' ring out with great clarity (*PV* 23).[32]

A preponderance of these long, heavily stressed monosyllables slows down the line and gives *Third Person* its unique rhythm and characteristic movement. English accentual-syllabic metrics prohibit frequent contiguous stresses such as we find in *Third Person*, but by the late 1930s the 'back of the iambic pentameter' had already been broken. Coffey had well-developed views on the subject and with Denis Devlin had formed the conclusion that verse could be analysed in 'terms of patterns of stresses'. This allowed both of them to dispense with the notion of metrical feet.[33] Whether or not one chooses to accept Coffey's views on this matter, his verse is only susceptible to scansion if one is prepared to immerse oneslf in the mire of Greek prosody. Units like the cretic and bacchiac can be identified but to examine Coffey's verse in this way would result in the kind of convoluted analysis that he himself rejected after reading Saintsbury's *History of English Prosody*.

Some lines do scan conveniently into iambs yet never with enough regularity to constitute a metrical base against which variants can be counterpointed. Placement of stress is determined by the sense of the line but given the ambiguous nature of the language and the lack of punctuation this will often depend on the reader's interpretation. A line or a stanza yields subtle nuances of emphasis and tone when it offers a choice of where to place the stress:

When she is sleeping find her

if you see with your eyes

(*PV* 34)

By placing the stress on 'she' an iambic pulse is set in motion in which case 'she' and 'you' acquire an increased specificity and the voice takes on an intimate tone, one appropriate to the communication of advice through a shared code. On the other hand, if the poem were isolated from the rest of the collection and read in the following way the symbolism would dissolve into irony, opening up a distance between the speaker and the auditor.

> When she is sleeping find her
>
> if you see with your eyes

In *Third Person* the end-stopped line is treated as the basic unit of meaning. Lines rarely end with conjunctions or subjects that point towards an ensuing predicate. This paradigm is well established in the earlier poems so that when Coffey does depart from it the result is genuinely impressive. Apollinaire, whose works Coffey had translated, frequently uses the same device in his longer poems. 'Patience No Memory', which is preceded by a poem whose concluding lines are emphatically end-stopped, opens with two consecutively enjambed lines so that the verse acquires a dramatic force similar to the opening of some of Donne's songs or sonnets.

The opening stanzas of 'Thirst' offer a good example of Coffey's ability to create subtle contrasts of rhythm and movement while maintaining a constant interval between stresses. Note how the space between the two stanzas is the temporal equivalent of a single stressed syllable:

> Horror dies for glazed eyes
> when the fish has fought the hook
>
> The floating reed shall swell and sink
> and sink and shall not cease
> from sinking
> green stone red weed
> hands met in night light
>
> (PV 31)

Apart from the sound patterning, what makes the opening two lines so memorable is the way the beat is maintained while the stress pattern is first pulled back and then thrown forwards to create a cohesive unit held together in a balanced tension. Coffey springs a surprise in the fifth line by playing sense against rhythm. The anticipation of closure created by the repetition of the four/three stress pattern of the compact opening unit is reinforced by the way the fourth line supplies a rhythm that closely parallels the second.[34] Expectations seem to be fulfilled until the reader discovers that 'cease' functioned as a transitive verb, its end-stopped sense seen in retrospect as a mirage. The effect nicely conveys the continued downward motion of the sinking reed which comes to a halt on the heavily stressed monosyllables of the sixth line. The beat is maintained but a lack of unstressed syllables arrests movement.

Bearing this in mind then, puzzlement at how to read lines composed entirely out of stressed monosyllables can be dispelled if the reader accepts that a pause the equivalent of an unstressed silent syllable can often separate two contiguous stresses. Analysed metrically one could say that each of the pronouns in the second line of the following quotation from 'Third Person' is the equivalent of the trochees in the third line.

> She finds pain
> he she we you they
> this one that one
> other the same
>
> (PV 36)

I end this brief discussion of the rhythms of *Third Person* by stating simply that they are like nothing else in Irish poetry. Critics could object to Coffey's apparent willingness to rely on metre rather than speech-stress to provide the necessary fourth stress in some of the lines of 'A Drop of Fire', yet the same criticism was levelled at Coleridge's *Christabel*. Others could take exception to the way Coffey's irregular rhythms impede a 'lyrical flow', which is, in a way, akin to denouncing Webern for his failure to provide nicely contoured melodies. What defines *Third Person* as a collection is the way all its elements are dedicated to a specific project. In its deliberate yet varying rhythms one senses the conviction of a poet who has discovered a mode of expression that possesses its own entelechy, one that is adequate to his own private and exacting aesthetic.

The cast of Coffey's rhythm has much to do with his syntactic style which is characterised by unfamiliar juxtapositions of simple nouns, verbs, pronouns and prepositions; function words are kept to a minimum. A comparison of finished poems and early drafts reveals a search for greater concision.[35] Like Mallarmé, Coffey was fond of ellipsis and he employs different species of it in *Third Person*: important conjunctions between words (*brachylogia*) and clauses (*asyndeton*) are omitted. Syllepsis, the yoking of one verb to two objects or subjects, is used in this example from 'Spurred' to project a state of feeling into images of nature's beauty and abundance: 'If he turns/ glazed skies go gold/ and fields' (*PV*30). By suppressing important auxiliary verbs in

'Dedication' Coffey invites the reader to consider eyes as both the organs and the objects of perception.

In this respect of syntax, interesting comparisons can be made with other contemporary poets, for instance the American, George Oppen. Coffey, Oppen and to a lesser extent the aforementioned Basil Bunting, defined their positions by resisting the type of modernism that prevailed in their respective countries.[36] For these poets 'making it new' was a process of reduction, an ability to work with the most basic elements a test of authenticity.

Oppen's *Discrete Series*, which was published four years before *Third Person*, possesses a syntax that is positively telegraphic compared to Coffey's, as this description of the movement of an elevator shows:

> Up
> Down.     Round
> Shiny fixed
> Alternatives
>
> From the quiet
>
> Stone floor . . .[37]

The asceticism that marks the style of both poets is evident in their implicit faith in the efficacy of small words. The difficulties that *Third Person* and *Discrete Series* present can rarely be resolved by consulting a dictionary.[38] Oppen's objectivist aesthetic, which expressed itself as a concern with 'the substantive, with the subject of the sentence' resulted in a style which is characterised by a poverty of predicates.[39] In the rarefied world of *Third Person*, too, language loses many of the forms considered indispensable to normal discourse: punctuation, proper nouns, adverbs of manner and important conjunctions like 'because' rarely feature. Although the scaled down forms of both *Third Person* and *Discrete Series* imply a shared antipathy towards the high style of early modernism, it would seem that Coffey and Oppen could not differ more on the issue of what poetry could feasibly say.

I have discussed how Coffey tries to take language beyond the empirically verifiable world in order to examine universal patterns that inhere in human relationships while simultaneously implying an ideal code against which these patterns can be tested. This metaphysical and theological dimension is something Oppen would have detested, however. There are historical references in *Discrete Series*, but the past can only be invoked through the immediately visible, like a painting by Fragonard.[40] Oppen, like Heidegger, was preoccupied by the mystery of 'presentness', and the fragmented forms of *Discrete Series* register the wonder and the shock of common experience. Unlike *Third Person*, there is an almost skintight closeness of fit between the way we perceive the physical world and the words that present it. The structures of conventional grammar do not reflect the world as Oppen sees it and he dismantles them and then reassembles them into his own grammar of unmediated perception. Poetry was a test of sincerity – 'actualness is prosody'– and its success could be measured empirically.[41] Oppen's scope of vision was determined by what he could see, his vocabulary delimited by what he alone could truthfully say:

> Thus
> Hides the
>
> Parts—the prudery
> Of Frigidaire, of
> Soda-jerking ———
>
> Thus
>
> Above the
>
> Plane of lunch, of wives
> Removes itself
>
> . . . . . .
>
> big-Business[42]

Interesting contrasts can be made between the way Oppen and Coffey bring their respective aesthetics to bear on the smallest unit of meaning. The space underneath the fragment 'Above the' conveys the time it takes for the eye to move through the space that separates the soda-fountain from the 'Plane of lunch'. The pace of the poem is dictated by the mode of perception, form is determined by the 'ineluctable modality of the visible.'[43]

Coffey, on the other hand, employs prepositions to spatialise and impose a shape on what Eliot called 'the general mess of imprecision of feeling'.[44] The reader is continually presented with formulations in which abstract nouns rather than proper or common nouns are governed by a preposition with the result that these abstractions seem to take on a spatial dimension: 'there was patience in my need' (*PV 25*), 'beyond her small will' (*PV 31*), and 'She lives in pure loss alone'(*PV 34*). Feelings and emotions are treated as items that can be lost or found: 'You shall not find to give her/ the form of touch she needs' (*PV 34*) and 'She finds pain' (*PV 36*). They possess the accidents of physical objects: 'red as anger/ white as pain' (*PV 33*). By systematically inverting those deep structures of grammar that set concrete entities over against abstractions, the verse cuts across the numbing drift of language and objectifies inner states of feeling in a way that lends them a hard-edged palpability and rawness.

One of the intriguing features of these spare poems is how easily they accomodate a diverse range of voices that includes Dante, Milton, Samuel Ferguson and T.S. Eliot. It is often difficult to say with any real conviction whether these other voices are simply fragments which have been detached from their original bases and unwittingly stored up as echoes in the poet's ear or whether they are allusions used with conscious intention. John Hollander proposes a useful hierarchy of allusive modes ranging from actual quotation, to allusion – which may be periphrastic or fragmentary – and finally, echo.[45]

The fragment from Dante's *Purgatorio* towards the end of 'The Enemy' does not qualify as a quotation because it is only a fragment; it is an important allusion, however. The line from 'A Drop of Fire', 'Turn the maledictive stones', is merely an echo, the source of which can be traced to one of Samuel Ferguson's *Lays of the Western Gael*.[46] This bears no special thematic relevance to Coffey's poem and I think it can be safely assumed that it found its way into 'A Drop of Fire' simply because Coffey liked the sound of it.

The snatches of Eliot heard in 'Spurred' and 'Gentle' are arguably allusions because their specific sources both express a condition of spiritual poverty as an imagined state of death-in-life.[47] In the context of *Third Person* they do not signify a modern crisis, and the implication is that, despite the particular inflection that a specific time may give a state of feeling, such states are constant throughout human history. More significantly *Third Person*, unlike *The Waste Land* and *The Hollow Men*, does hold out the prospect of divine grace. 'T.S. Eliot understands nothing about grace', Coffey once remarked in a letter written to Thomas MacGreevy.[48]

When echoes of a particular poet tend to cluster in a single poem and when they bear on its theme, as they do in 'A Drop of Fire', one can safely assume that they function as allusions. The title alone calls up Milton's images of 'liquid fire' and 'burning lakes' while simultaneously playing on two senses of 'drop'. A reference to 'a garden farthest back' (*PV* 29) cannot avoid evoking Edenic associations. The penultimate stanza repeats the famous metaphor of 'blind mouths' from *Lycidas*, a poem with several references to rising and falling stars. Besides calling up images of falling and sinking, these allusions reinforce Coffey's identification of male figures with stars. 'A Drop of Fire', then, is Coffey's version of the Fall. It describes a descent from the calmly observed heavens to a private hell, and from a union of two to an extreme state of alienation.

Two important allusions help lend some focus to the mysterious female figure in 'The Enemy'. Most readers will recognise the final line of the first stanza – 'ranging in continual change' (*PV* 32) – as an allusion to Wyatt's 'They Flee from Me' in which the fickleness of woman is the ground of the speaker's complaint. The fragment from *Purgatorio* Canto XIX is sung by a deformed hag who appears in Dante's dream, transforms into a figure of beauty under his gaze and identifies herself as the siren who led mariners astray such was the sweetness of her singing:

> 'Io son', cantava, 'io son dolce serena,
> che' marinari in mezzo mar dismago
> tanto son di piacere a sentir piena![']⁴⁹

With typical economy, Coffey, supposing that the reader will have identified the context of the source, breaks off abruptly and substitutes the latin '*Coeli*' for Dante's 'io son dolce serena'. Beatrice and the Siren, female embodiments of good and evil respectively, are simultaneously glimpsed in a double exposure as polarised expressions of a single female principle. This is directly relevant to a poem whose subject continually eludes formulation in words but more importantly it relates the poem to one of the principal themes of *Third Person*, namely multiplicity in unity.

An earlier section discussed Coffey's application of this concept to human relationships, but I want to examine briefly the question of whether and how *Third Person* can reconcile this concept of distinction in unity to its implicit Christian ethos. The final stanza of 'Third Person' is hugely important in this respect and it throws the whole collection into a new light.

> Who shall bend
> sails white wings
> the sun with the sea
> soothe them with south hand
> until ice melt
> heart flame
> rains of fulfilment
> bless the cedar tree
>
> (*PV* 37)

It begins like a question but 'soothe' and 'bless' could also be read as imperative or optative verbs and as the stanza progresses it seems to incline more towards the condition of prayer. Christian symbolism abounds: the 'south hand' refers to the south wind that brings heat, melts ice and causes rain. It is a recurring symbol of the agency of the Holy Spirit throughout the Bible particularly in the New Testament and the Epistles. The line 'rains of fulfilment' echoes Psalm 72:6 which expresses the hope that a just and peaceful king will be like 'rain that falls on the mown grass, like showers that water the earth!' The 'cedar tree' mentioned in Solomon 5:15 is commonly accepted as a prefiguration of the coming Christ. God, therefore, manifests himself through a creative, dynamic principle – the 'south hand' – by whose operation all opposites are fruitfully reconciled. What is being described is the Christian mystery of the Holy Trinity in which the 'Holy Spirit proceeds from the mutual love of the Father and the Son'.[50]

Coleridge developed his 'logosophic system' out of Giordano Bruno's argument that the creative principle of all life had its source in the dynamic relationships that inhered in the Trinity. Coleridge's system is based on a formulation of the Father as Absolute Thesis which recognises itself in the reality of the Son or Absolute Antithesis. Both terms are reconciled into an Absolute Synthesis of Love, the Holy Spirit. This whole system is grounded on an antecedent fourth term or Absolute Prothesis which signifies the Absolute Will and 'is essentially causative of reality, essentially & absolutely . . . boundless from without and from within.'[51] This Prothesis therefore introduces an 'ipseity . . . alterity' relationship which is the source of all reality and of the systems of relationships of sameness and difference operative in it. Human love, by which the opposition of two individuals is reconciled into a synthesis, mirrors this distinction-in-unity which finds perfect expression in the Trinity. Coleridge went so far as to formulate marriage in terms similar to his analysis of the Trinity. Love was the third term or 'bi-polar line' of a reciprocal relationship in which the husband was the 'Positive Pole or Thesis; the Wife the Negative or Antithesis'.[52]

I am not suggesting that Coffey's identification of the Trinity as the spring and origin of all human relations is owing to the influence of Coleridge. For one thing, much of Coleridge's philosophical writing was not available in published form in 1938. But I do believe that Coleridge's thinking about concepts such as the Trinity, sameness and difference, love and society, spells out much that is implicit in *Third Person*.

Apart from its aesthetic merit, what makes *Third Person* much more than an arid treatise is the way language itself is treated as the means and the ground of enquiry. The ambiguity latent in a single word is itself a powerful metaphor of the 'many-in-one', as is the voice which speaks these poems. The frequent shuttling between singular and plural pronouns in a poem like 'A Drop of Fire' is an innovative way of invoking the concept of the individual and class as it arises in human relations and it interrogates the concept of shared essences that such metaphysical systems of classification necessarily presuppose.

Coffey's quest for the timeless, then, does not start in the physical world but in language itself. The poems do not feature staged moments of

privileged vision, which I believe is a refreshing and brave departure for a
poet whose deepest sensibilities are ultimately lyrical. It is for this reason
that *Third Person* does not present as many points of attack to the
would-be poststructuralist as, say, some of the work of Thomas
MacGreevy. Coffey never deploys the questionable rhetorical strategies of
'Anglo-Irish', a poem which is less an unmasking of essential differences
and 'stranger ways' than a projection of its author's private anxieties
and historically conditioned animosities.[53]

*Third Person*, on the other hand, seems to delight in subverting its own
discourse. It openly acknowledges the extent to which suasive rhetoric
depends more on context and performance than on semantic content.
Does the penultimate stanza of 'Amaranth' constitute a rebuke or is it in
fact an invitation? Is the shadowy third person a benign or a threatening
presence? Is this mysterious three-way relationship a variation on the
eternal triangle archetype or does it symbolise the mystery of the Trinity?
The poems are calculated to confront the reader with such questions and
it is precisely at those moments when such questions form in the mind
that deeper levels of meaning begin to reveal themselves.

The most curious and baffling paradox of all is that the very devices
that Coffey employs in his quest for truth – riddle, an acute awareness of
the conditions of textuality (as in the title 'White'), intertextuality, the
interpenetration of opposites, paradox and playful ambiguity – are those
very things that the sceptical poststructuralist prizes most in literature.
Moreover, in order to dismantle the concepts transmitted by *Third
Person*, s/he must first connect the poems to them by making imaginative
stretches of interpretation. This, of course, involves validating terms that
the poststructuralist is obliged to refute. In short, any strong reading of
*Third Person* is destined to be a misreading. Some feminist critics might
object to the construction of gender in a poem like 'Amaranth', but if he
were alive, Coffey could feasibly argue that 'fram[ing] a lilac quilt'
functions not as a metonym for woman's work but rather as a metaphor
for 'making' poems.

J.C.C. Mays calls attention to a wit and a gaiety in these poems: and
like much else in *Third Person*, this element can be enjoyed without
recourse to books of philosophy or theology.[54] Words flicker into life in
the most novel ways and syllables enjoy a rare autonomy. Notice how the
context of 'splendour' in this line draws attention to its second syllable
whose meaning cuts right against the sense of the word of which it forms
a part: 'Her bitter splendour green eyes/. . .' (*PV* 34). The oblique way in
which some titles relate to their respective poems has been mentioned, but
it is intriguing to think that an amateur gardener with little interest in
poetry would possibly spot the relevance of the title 'Amaranth'– a

Brian Coffey, Untitled, 1978. Lithograph, 22 cm. x 16 cm. Number 1 of 6. The first 25 copies of *Third Person* were illustrated with an original engraving by S.W. Hayter. Coffey developed an interest in lithography later in his life. This untitled lithograph, which dates from 1978, shows that his love of ambiguity could also express itself visually.

garden flower more commonly known as 'love-lies-bleeding'– before the
scholar who would probably fix his/her attention solely on the meaning it
possesses in academic discourse.[55]

I have said earlier that Coffey was essentially a lyric poet and I suggest
that when read in the order in which they are arranged the poems are felt
as parts of an embracing lyrical structure. The opening lines of 'White'
and 'One Way' are useful points of reference by which we can measure
the distance through which the the collection has taken us (PV 24, 38).
The poems seem to have been written as parts of a larger unit in much the
same way that the poems in Oppen's Discrete Series were conceived as
integers in a mathematical series.

Poems continually strike echoes from previous poems and sound new
motifs that will be picked up later on, so that Third Person possesses a
degree of organic unity that is not usual in the conventional poetry
collection. For this reason I think that M. L. Rosenthal and Sally M.
Gall's defintion of the modern sequence 'as a grouping of mainly lyrical
poems, rarely uniform in pattern, which tend to interact as an organic
whole', best describes the genre of Third Person.[56] This preoccupation
with form befits a scholar who took as the subject of his doctoral thesis
the notion of order according to St Thomas Aquinas. Of all the Europa
poets, Coffey was the only one to seize the opportunity to stake a claim
for the 'poetry collection' to be considered as a genre in itself. That Third
Person amounts to an exploration of the formal possibilities available within
a collection is signalled in the opening poem. Rather than inscribe his
'dedication' on the fly-leaf, Coffey makes an important gesture by turning
it into a poem that is relevant to the concerns of the book as a whole.

The next poem, 'White', establishes the conceptual framework upon
which later poems will build while reflecting back on 'Dedication'. The
three poems that follow 'White' form a grouping that moves in
accordance with Earl Miner would call a 'principle of fluctuating
relation'.[57] 'Amaranth' and 'I Can Not See . . . ' do not advance a plot but
are interrelated through the recurring figure of the sea-faring male. Both
poems possess the 'cognitive constituents' of a narrative but the identity
of these constituents changes. For example, the remarkable effect by
which a third person is insinuated into the dramatic situation of 'Amaranth'
is achieved differently in the following poem. The third poem of this
grouping, the choric 'All We Have', comments on what has beeen said
and done in the two previous poems but the voice has changed from 'I' to
'We'. Coffey added 'Women Kind:' to the beginning of the title in Poems
and Versions. The enlarged title echoes the lines 'mine the black light/ that
drives kind to kind' (PV 26) of the previous poem, which suggests that
'we' includes those who have been 'drive[n]' to their own kind. Taken as

a discrete sub-section the sequence implies that the forces that separate people and sever relationships paradoxically create new formations.

The next pair of poems is an ironic juxtaposition. The relative equanimity with which the speaker of 'Content' delivers five self-contained and loosely related aphorisms about the brevity of life and the importance of making 'an act of love' contrasts sharply with the dramatic movement and emotional range of the next poem. The insertion of the unproblematical 'Content' into a grouping of poems that is marked by discordancy and alienation introduces variety into a broader emotional rhythm that would otherwise be monotonous. 'A Drop of Fire', which occupies a central position in *Third Person*, introduces a new set of images and rhythms: stars, water and its reflective properties, rhythms of rising and falling or sinking, and contrasts of stasis and movement are all worked into the next batch of poems. This grouping culminates in 'Patience No Memory', a veritable echo chamber that resonates strongly with at least five preceding poems.

'Third Person' sounds a new note of philosophical detachment after the emotional turbulence of the middle poems and together with 'One Way' makes up a balanced pair. The tentative question-cum-prayer that ends the penultimate poem provides a context in which the forthright indicative lines of 'One Way' are not only understood as a celebration of a new clarity of vision but also as an affirmation of spiritual renewal brought about by the gift of divine grace. It is important to emphasise that this added dimension is very much a function of the position of the poem. The sense of expectancy created by 'Third Person' exerts a pull on 'One Way' and draws out its latent symbolic meaning. If it were read in isolation, the existential argument of 'One Way'– the importance of embracing the dialectical quality of life – would occlude its latent religious significance. Coffey ends where many others might begin and it seems fitting that *Third Person* should conclude by recording a moment of departure. It is also worth noting that in its broad movement *Third Person* anticipates later works like *Missouri Sequence* and *Advent*.

In his overview of the tendentious definitions that different critical schools have imposed on the lyric, Mark Jeffreys identifies the values upheld by the champions of postmodernism, values that render post-modernists inimical to the lyric as they understand it. A postmodernist poetics, he writes, emphasises the following qualities:

> . . . openness in place of closure, intertextuality in place of the individual text, a fiction of polyvocality in place of the fiction of the 'speaker', and the appearance of subversive play in place of the appearance of ironic control . . . [.][58]

Many contemporary commentators argue from the premise that the specific cultural, economic and historical conditions out of which many Irish poets, dramatists and novelists wrote are reflected in a literature that abounds in the aforementioned qualities. It is odd, then, that they should overlook such a wonderfully inventive work as *Third Person*. I believe that this neglect of Coffey's early achievement reveals a blind spot in current thinking about Irish writing and it points up the all too frequent failure of Irish critics to cherish one of their own in advance of resounding international approval. Coffey's best critics are British and American. It is time for Irish readers to peer beyond the anthology pieces and discover for themselves the full diversity of Irish modernism.

# 3

# COFFEY'S METHOD
# OF TRANSLATION

We appear to have a clearer notion of what qualifies a translation for approbation than what makes a particular poem good or bad. Translations are deemed worthy if they are fluent, idiomatic and natural sounding. The other benchmark of success is transparency, the creation of the illusion that the translation is not a translation but an original poem. Most translators continue to proceed on the asssumption that fluency and transparency are ideals to which they must aspire, hence the title of Lawrence Venuti's comprehensive history of the development of the dominant Anglo-American model of translation, *The Translator's Invisibility*. It is not surprising, then, that translators who do not conform to this prescribed model and who insist on maintaining their 'visibility' do not receive the type of critical attention that their work deserves.

Readers unfamiliar with alternative models of translation will be struck by the opaque quality of Brian Coffey's versions. By allowing his English to absorb the rhythms and syntax of the language in which the poem is written, in this case French, Coffey signifies the foreignness of the original. Because he does not seek to domesticate the poem and make it assume values that are determined by the standards of current English usage, Coffey will not win the approbation of those who unquestioningly accept the received view of the translator's task – a view which if analysed and examined in its historical and cultural contexts will be seen to have been shaped more by political and economic interests than by purely literary considerations. Rather than provide a clear paraphrase nicely tricked up in an imitative rhyme scheme, Coffey excavates the original and attends to meanings that reside beneath the immediate surface of the poem. For this reason, his translations possess a dimension that most others lack. This chapter aims to substantiate this argument by examining his versions of important works by Rimbaud and Nerval, and his extraordinary translation of Mallarmé's *Un Coup de dés*.

What I say above about rhyme schemes does not imply that they are mere surface details – inessential features that translators must discard if they are to get at the essential core of the poem. On the contrary, a rhyme scheme is much more than an abstract pattern that can be separated from the poem and reconstituted in a foreign language; the way a rhyme scheme provides patterns of meaning is unique to the poem and specific to the language in which the poem is written. It is arguable that the translator who wishes to render something of the way rhymes function in the original work ought to consult an alternative model of translation, such as that of Celia and Louis Zukofsky, who sought to present translations that matched the actual sounds of the original poem. Coffey, I am sure, would have agreed with Nabokov who conceded that the original poem when shorn of its rhyme scheme would not be able to 'soar and to sing'; however, the original could be 'nicely dissected and mounted, and scientifically studied in all its organic details.'[1]

Coffey's translations do not soar, nor do they sing, as a comparison of his version of Rimbaud's 'Le Bateau ivre' ('The Joy-Mad Ship') with Samuel Beckett's will demonstrate. At first reading a Coffey version will have the appearance of a slavish, word-for-word rendering and careless readers will dismiss it as a mere crib. It is perhaps worth noting that Hölderlin's translations of Sophocles, which are now regarded as classics of German literature, were dismissed in the nineteenth century because he moulded German around the syntactic structures of the original Greek; in fact, his literal rendering of Greek syntax was often achieved at the expense of meaning. Frequently Coffey will insert an ungainly phrase, and sometimes his translation of a French word or phrase intentionally deviates from the sense intended by the poet.[2] The lexicon of his translations is not defined by modern usage: archaisms, foreign words and nonce words also feature.

Those who would attribute the oddities of Coffey's translations to incompetence need to be reminded of his academic credentials. Coffey lived and studied in France for many years. He could speak French more fluently than Denis Devlin and Samuel Beckett. He specialised in Thomistic philosophy which required a mastery of Latin and a knowledge of classical Greek. His doctoral thesis was written in French and he conducted much of his correspondence through that language. The reviews he wrote for Eliot's *The Criterion* reveal an encyclopaedic knowledge of French literature, especially nineteenth-century poetry, much of which he had committed to memory. Moreover, from the time he was a schoolboy he was fascinated by the challenge of translation, and the MacGreevy papers contain some early translations from the Latin of Petronius that would be deemed acceptable by conventional standards.[3]

What is the point, then, of this affected clumsiness and why do his translations seem calculated to reflect the conditions of the act of translating? Coffey, as I have argued, was not interested in creating the illusion that his translations were original utterances. A skilled linguist, who thought deeply about the act of translation, Coffey was acutely aware that no translation could achieve true semantic equivalence and that every translation was an interpretation. Coffey had his own clearly defined set of values but he was capable of admiring the poems of others even though he did not share the values and assumptions that informed those poems. Rather than smuggle his own values into his translations, he inscribes them in a manifest way. A Coffey 'version', then, is unique because it marks a creative and unusually intense engagement with the original text and for this reason different criteria ought to be applied when we come to appraise it.

A careful reading of *Dice Thrown Never Will Annul Chance*, his translation of Mallarmé's *Un Coup de dés jamais n'abolira le hasard*, will show how Coffey highlights the values and arguments of that work by subtly testing them against his own. Mallarmé's speculations, propositions and hypotheses are subjected to intense scrutiny and Coffey carefully, but not obtrusively, inscribes his response to them by skillfully suggesting alternatives; his translation of the title phrase and his disposal of it across the poem are cases in point. Coffey does not seek to negate the argument of the original work nor does he want to assimilate it into his own argument: it is simply a matter of suggesting another set of values that do not inhere in the poem. This is something that will be examined in greater detail later.

It is important to bear in mind that most of Coffey's translations or versions, as he preferred to call them, were also intended as aids for 'other Irish poets' to help them 'on their their difficult paths'. Because many of the larger publishers still regard translation as a second-rate activity, translators are under an added pressure to provide fluent, 'user-friendly' texts. Coffey was under no such pressure and he generally relied on smaller, more sympathetic publishers or university presses to print his work. Many of the commercially available translations smooth over the complex turns of mind of a poet like Mallarmé. While they display much ingenuity in imitating his rhyme schemes they are often characterised by a spurious clarity.

The point is that Coffey did not regard translation as some kind of plate-spinning trick. The qualities of the original that Coffey tries to render in his translations are the very qualities that lend his own poetry its distinctive cast – namely rhythm, syntax and complexity of thought and feeling. His rhythms are generally determined by those of the original. He does not feel obliged to convert alexandrines into iambic pentameters.

Caesurae, enjambments and accents are retained where possible so that Coffey's lines carefully follow the movement of the French. By foregoing any attempt to imitate rhyme schemes, Coffey affords himself the freedom to focus on the task of suggesting the densities of thought and complexities of feeling embedded in the original poem. Consequently, his translations can be challenging. They are at least as difficult as the original texts, but they always repay careful study. One finds that the ambiguities in a poem like Rimbaud's 'Le Bateau ivre', ambiguities which have given rise to many pages of critical debate, are also present in Coffey's version. These ambiguities are suppressed in Samuel Beckett's headlong translation which features many marvellous moments but does so at the expense of missing the vital mystery inherent in the original. A comparison of how the two translate the opening stanzas – quoted below – will illustrate the point.

> Comme je descendais des Fleuves impassibles,
> Je ne me sentis plus guidé par les haleurs:
> Des Peaux-Rouges criards les avaient pris pour les cibles,
> Les ayant cloués nus aux poteaux de couleurs
>
> J'étais insoucieux de tous les équipages,
> Porteur de blés flamands ou de cotons anglais.
> Quand avec mes haleurs ont fini ces tapages,
> Les fleuves m' ont laissé descendre où je voulais.[4]

> (Rimbaud)

> Downstream on impassive rivers suddenly
> I felt the towline of the boatmen slacken.
> Redskins had taken them in a scream and stripped them and
> Skewered them to the glaring stakes for targets.
>
> Then, delivered from my straining boatmen,
> From the trivial racket of trivial crews and from
> The freights of Flemish grain and English cotton,
> I made my own course down the passive rivers.[5]

> (Beckett)

It is clear that Beckett intended his translation to be understood as the narrative of a voyage that has taken place and that the sensations and visions that will follow have already been experienced and witnessed. He has altered Rimbaud's rhythms to inject a greater sense of excitement and movement into the verse. In the original stanzas all the corresponding lines are end-stopped but Beckett introduces significant enjambments in lines 1, 3 and 6. The insertion of added conjunctions and the elimination of Rimbaud's caesurae speed up the tempo. His employment of alliteration which lends the verse an added vividness is certainly remarkable. Over the course of the next twenty stanzas in which the boat relates details of its voyage, Beckett gives free rein to his large vocabulary as he suddenly veers between the lyricism of, 'In spumes of flowers I have risen from my anchors/And canticles of wind have blessed my wings' to the more demotic, '. . . screeching birds/ Flaxen-eyed, shiteing on my trembling decks . . .'.

Such juxtapostions of the beautiful and the unsavoury are, of course, an attempt to capture an essential element of Rimbaud's style, his 'parade sauvage'. Yet Beckett, as we shall soon see, has committed himself to an interpretation that suggests he was influenced by 'la fable de Rimbaud'. Beckett, who loved Rimbaud's poetry, wrote this translation when he was a young man and it is clear that he understood and appreciated the poem as an expression of disdain for the 'trivial racket of trivial crews'. Perhaps he might have translated the poem differently had he the benefit of the advice of Étiemble, a 'back-to-the-text' critic who believed that the myth of Rimbaud had been responsible for a distorted understanding of the French poet's work:

> 'Lisez Rimbaud. Un passage vous résiste? Prenez votre grammaire et le Littré . . . Si . . . au mythe d'un écrivain nous préférons sa vérité, procurons des éditions, et les plus minutieuses et les plus critiques du monde . . .'[6]

Coffey's translation of the opening stanzas is far more measured; there are no fireworks. The movement of the lines hugs the contours of the original and his careful rendering of key phrases makes several interpretive possibilities available. The ambiguities of these stanzas are the key to a reading of the poem that successsfully integrates the problematic last stanzas into the whole. Coffey's version is the only one that I know of that provides that key:

> As I was moving down unmoved Rivers
> I felt me no longer guided by the haulers:
> screaming Redskins had taken them as targets,
> nailed them they had naked to painted poles.
>
> I was regardless of any crew or ship,
> freighter of Flemish wheat or English cotton.
> When with my haulers the racket was done
> the Rivers let me move down as I fancied.[7]

Some will object to Coffey's rendering of 'Je ne me sentis plus guidé. . .' in line 2 and argue that the second pronoun is unnecessary and ugly. The literalism is intentional because it suggests that all that follows is an imagined experience. This ambiguity is maintained in the second stanza.

Rimbaud's 'insoucieux de' and Coffey's 'regardless of' (here meaning 'heedless of') both hold out the possibility that the crew and the other vessels are still in the vicinity. Caught up in its own imaginary voyage, the boat has simply become unaware of them. 'Racket' could refer to the din of the Indian ambush or to the more mundane racket of freighting the boat; 'fancied' simultaneously conveys the enjoyment of an actual freedom and the pleasures of an imagined freedom.

In the following stanzas Coffey does not give himself the latitude that Beckett needs in order to pull off his flashes of brilliance. Instead, his version moves with the original and accumulates significant details along the way, details that bear on the meaning of Rimbaud's allegory. The balanced hemistichs of this line from stanza VIII contain an important set of oppositions that Beckett does not care to bring out:

> Et j'ai vu quelquefois ce que l'homme a cru voir!

> And my eyes have fixed phantasmagoria.
>
> > (Beckett)

> and there are times I have seen what man has thought to see!
>
> > (Coffey)

Coffey's version preserves an opposition that contrasts different modes of seeing and differentiates the boat from man. The line is important because it supports an allegorical reading which relates to the French poet's theory of *voyance*. In a famous letter to his former schoolmaster, Georges Izambard, Rimbaud argued that a poet had to undergo 'le dérèglement de *tous les sens*' in order to experience a more profound vision. This short excerpt from the letter provides a good gloss for the line: 'Je veux être poète, et je travaille à me rendre *Voyant*: vous ne comprendrez pas du tout'.[8]

In stanza XXI, Beckett, intent on creating a version that moves towards an unequivocal rejection of 'Europe's waters', is obliged to mistranslate Rimbaud's 'Je regrette l'Europe aux anciens parapets!' as 'I . . ./ Now remember Europe and her ancient ramparts.' Interestingly, Derek Mahon's reduced but very fine adaptation gives the line a sense that mingles memory and regret: 'But now, my ears/ Weary of this crescendo of sensations,/ I thought of Europe and its ancient towers.'[9] It would not have changed the metre if Mahon had translated the line in question as 'I longed for Europe and its ancient towers' in which case the values 'longed for' would be bound up in Europe's history. Coffey, on the other hand, gives 'I hanker for Europe its ancient keeping walls!' Here we can see the benefits of reading a translator who is alive to the innermost subtleties of a poem. Both Mahon and Beckett, by substituting 'and' for 'aux', have not differentiated between modern Europe and a Europe regarded retrospectively. In other words, Europe is understood as contemporary Europe with its repository of artefacts. Coffey's literal translation correctly identifies the complex feeling expressed by the boat – namely, a yearning for a *past* both personal and historical.[10]

Furthermore, Mahon's and Beckett's interpretations are based on the assumption that a physical distance separates the boat and modern Europe, an assumption which involves the suppression of a vital ambiguity. The original text and Coffey's translation retain the possibility that the boat has yet to undertake this voyage and that the 'eau d'Europe', as Marshall Lindsay convincingly argues, 'is not a place the boat may return to but the place in which it must remain if it does not set out on its fabulous adventure.'[11]

Two points need to be made before proceeding further. Earlier in this chapter I referred to Coffey's use of deviant translation and it might be argued that one cannot make a case for Coffey and charge Beckett for taking the same liberty, especially when both seem to mistranslate the word 'parapets'. I would suggest, however, that the phrase 'ancient keeping walls' is sufficiently odd to remind most readers that they are reading a translation and not an original poem. Coffey has employed a favourite device, one that he uses to great effect in his translation of *Un Coup de dés*. He has returned to the root of the word (*parapetto*: Italian for 'chest high wall') and translated an element of it back into English. 'Keeping', with its medieval associations, gives the line an added historical dimension while pointing up the contrast between Europe, with its crumbling walls hopelessly endeavouring to contain ('keep') its past, and the self-destructive dissipation of the boat. It is worth examining the etymological diversity of this line because it contains words that have roots in most of those languages (Greek, Latin, Norse, German and French) that have contributed to the development of English. Such is the nature of Coffey's method of translation that the reader is continually made aware that English is constructed out of foreign materials. A stimulated awareness of this diachronic dimension of language enriches the meaning of the line but, more significantly, it is another way of inscribing foreignness into the translation.

The second point is related to the first. Beckett has radically altered the thrust of the original poem and it is arguable that his interpretation of it was shaped by a felt empathy with Rimbaud. Important elements, indeed much of the complexity of 'Le Bateau ivre' had to be sacrificed. This is not to imply a criticism of Beckett's version which is imaginative and exhilarating; my sole purpose here is to highlight the benefits of Coffey's method. But I would suggest that Beckett had projected into his interpretation a feeling that he considered to be essentially Rimbaldian. A poem like 'Le Bateau ivre' is much more complex than some imagined essence. Beckett, as I have stated, wishes to make the poem into a gesture of renunciation – which in a sense it is; however, the nature of its renunciation is more complex and more specific than Beckett's version would suggest. Rimbaud's poem amounts to more than an expression of unmotivated ennui.

I have laboured my analysis of the line in which the boat expresses a longing for Europe because it bears heavily on the meaning of the concluding stanzas. Why does the boat so carefully define a 'pool/ black and cold' as the only water it longs for and by implication reject Europe? One valid answer is that the boat is still situated in the waters of Europe. One simply has to look again at the second stanza of Coffey's translation. He has actually heightened the ambiguity of the poem by translating 'porteur' in a way that suggests that there are other vessels in the vicinity and that the boat is still situated in domestic waterways. This has the effect of casting the Indian ambush into the realm of fantasy. All that will be related has been 'fancied', a vision or 'voyant' of what is to come and this is a possibility that the original poem makes available. The desire for the 'black pool' with its association of childhood memories is an unrealizable wish.[12] Like the ancient Europe that the boat yearns for, it is locked away or 'kept' in the past .

The final stanza, then, is a description of the vessels that sail the seas of modern Europe: cotton clippers, military vessels and prison boats. Coffey brings out the unpleasant features of these vessels: they are proud, destructive and menacing, and their presence symbolises the new values of a commercial and belligerent Europe. These are the values that the boat ultimately rejects. Cut off from a past to which it cannot return and faced with a present that it 'can no longer' accept, the boat opts instead for a future that it has glimpsed in a vision, a future of incredible experiences but one that the boat knows will ultimately destroy it. Like the *voyant* poet, 'il finirait par perdre l'intelligence de ses visions'. As Lindsay correctly argues, the structure of the poem is cyclical: 'it ends literally at its beginning; it concludes with the choice that provokes its opening lines'.[13]

> I can no longer, bathed in your languors, waves,
> storm the wakes of the cotton clippers,
> nor breast the pride of flags and flames,
> nor float where the hulks screw me with horrible eyes.

Coffey's attention to the detail contained within the original stanza cited below is remarkable.

Je ne puis plus, baigné de vos langueurs, ô lames,
Enlever leur sillage aux porteurs de cotons,
Ni traverser l'orgueil des drapeaux et des flammes,
Ni nager sous les yeux horribles des pontons!

Many of the rhythmical features that make the original stanza such a fitting conclusion to 'Le Bateau ivre' are retained in the translation: the caesurae that suggest lassitude in the first line; the rhythms that convey forward movement in the next two; finally, the long syllables of the last line which convey the slow, careful movement of the boat as it passes beneath the surveying eyes of the 'pontons'.[14]

The last stanza also features a good example of Coffey's use of deviant translation. He has given 'flames' for Rimbaud's 'flammes' which is a technically correct translation of the word but not in the sense that Rimbaud uses it – namely, to signify a naval pennant. 'Flames' draws attention to the destructive intent of these proud, resplendent vessels and maintains the rhythmic pattern of the original line.[15] Coffey then reverses this technique by refusing to translate 'pontons' as 'pontoons' unlike Beckett, and gives instead the more specific 'hulks', which accurately renders the sense intended by Rimbaud's 'pontons'.[16] The verb 'screws', which has penal associations in English, metaphorically describes the rivetting 'eyes' or portholes of the 'hulks'.[17]

I have dwelt at length on Coffey's version of 'Le Bateau ivre' in order to illustrate his method of translation and to demonstrate the intensity of his concentration on the given poem. His deviant translations are not really mistranslations because they always mark a significant reponse to a specific event in the original text. Apart from conveying turns of mind that exist only in the French, Coffey's literalisms also point up the differences and the affinities that exist between the two languages. By way of deviant translation and literalism then, Coffey's text reflects the conditions of translation and such open declarations of presence earn him the right to expose and test the values implicit in the poem.

This analysis of 'The Joy-Mad Ship' incorporates some elements of Marshall Lindsay's imaginative but perceptive reading of 'Le Bateau ivre'. When applied to the translation, his interpretation, which is firmly rooted in a close analysis of the last four stanzas of the poem, reveals just how much of the ambiguity of the original Coffey succeeds in carrying over into his translation. This gift for capturing much of the complexity of a poem provides the 'linguistically challenged' reader with a rare insight into the peculiar modes of thought that distinguish French from, say, English or American poetry.

*     *     *

'The Joy-Mad Ship' was first published in 1975 in an issue of *Irish University Review* dedicated to Brian Coffey. The issue, which featured a large selection of his translations and much recent original poetry, also included a version of Nerval's 'El Desdichado'. Coffey's translation of the sequence to which the sonnet belongs was published by the English poet Fred Beake in 1985 and Nicholas Johnson has republished it in a recent volume of his *etruscan reader* series.

Unlike other translators of Nerval, Coffey retains all the mythical and obscure historical allusions that lend the poems their curiously medieval flavour. This medieval quality, also expressed in archaisms and inversions that would have seemed anachronistic to the nineteenth-century French reader and which Coffey renders in his translations, is important because Nerval was in a sense trying to reconnect the sonnet to its sixteenth-century roots. Neither the polished, elegant style of the Parnassians nor the impassioned eloquence of Romantics like Lamartine or Hugo could convey the tensions and complex feelings that Nerval wished to express. It is this complexity of feeling, a felt disparity between aspiration and achievement which continually expresses itself as a desire for synthesis, that Coffey captures so superbly. It is instructive to see how Coffey's deepening appreciation of 'El Desdichado' is reflected in the revisions he made to the early 1975 translation. The first and the later version are given below.

> I am the tenebrous one, widowed, disconsolate,
> Prince of Aquitania at the torn-down tower.
> My sole star is dead and my lute constellate
> bears the black sun of melancholia.
>
> In the night of the tomb, thou who didst comfort me,
> give me back Posillipo and the Italian sea,
> the flower which so won my heart desolated
> and vine-arbour where vine-shoot with rose allies.
>
> Am I Eros or Phoebus? . . . Lusignon or Biron?
> My brow is red yet from the kiss of the queen.
>
> I have dreamed in grotto where siren swims. . .
>
> And twice a conqueror have crossed Acheron
> inflecting turn about on Orpheus' lyre
> the sigh of the saint and the cry of the fay.

> (1975)

I am the tenebrous one – widowed – disconsolate,
Prince of Aquitania at the torn-down tower;
My sole star is dead, and my lute constellate
bears the black sun of Melancholia.

In the night of the tomb thou who didst console me
give me back Posilipo and the Italian sea,
flower which pleased so my heart desolated,
and vine arbour where vine-shoot with rose allies.

Am I Eros or Phoebus? Lusignan or Biron?
My brow is red yet from the kiss of the queen:
I have dreamed in grotto where siren swims. . . .

and twice a conqueror I have crossed Acheron:
inflecting turn about on Orpheus' lyre
The sighing of the saint and the cry of the fay.[18]

(1997)

The revision of line 1 has the effect of surrounding 'widowed' with silence, giving it an added significance that it lacked in the first version where it simply belonged to a set of adjectives. More importantly it breaks up the second part of the line so that its movement more closely resembles the limping rhythm of the corresponding passage in the original:

Je suis le ténébreux, – le veuf, – l'inconsolé,

The long pause after 'veuf' signalled a break with the traditional techniques of French versification, and the placement of the shortest of three terms in the middle of the line flouted all the rules of eloquence.[19] Coffey worked hard in order to get this essential feature – the strangeness, if you will – of the poem into his version. Like many other translators working in English, Derek Mahon plainly regards the iambic pentameter as a satisfactory equivalent for the alexandrine but we can see from his translation just how much rearrangement it took to arrive at a rendering that does not possess the depth of Coffey's version. The comma and the alliteration in the second half of the line divides it into two discrete units.

I am the widower – dim, disconsolate –[20]

Getting the movement and rhythm of this first line right was obviously a priority for the American poet Robin Blaser. His version of the sonnet makes wonderful use of space, something that Coffey would do later in his versions of Mallarmé's sonnets:

I am the Darkness    the Widowed    the Unconsoled,[21]

Coffey probably considered the comma in line 5 of the first version to be redundant because a natural pause between the two stressed syllables 'tomb' and 'thou' fulfills the same function. The substitution of 'console' for 'comfort' clarifies the opposition between the end-positions of this line and the first. Coffey's translation of this quatrain, which I give below, is worth considering in more detail because it captures many of the crucial tensions and ambiguities that I mentioned earlier.

> Dans la nuit du tombeau, toi qui m'as consolé,
> Rends-moi le Pausilippe et la mer d' Italie,
> La *fleur* qui plaisait tant à mon coeur désolé,
> Et la treille où la pampre à la rose s'allie.[22]

Apart from the identity of 'toi' an element of mystery centres around the phrase 'Dans la nuit du tombeau'. Is this 'night of the tomb' to be understood as a time and a place of consolation or, on the other hand, will it be a night of disinheritance or exile? Jacques Dhaenens, in a book-length study of the poem makes a convincing case for his argument that 'La nuit du tombeau est donc ambiguë: elle désole et elle console'.[23] Both of Coffey's versions contain this important ambiguity: the omission of the comma in the second actually heightens it.[24]

The revision of line 7 is without doubt the most important and it merits careful analysis. While it may seem clumsy, the degree of concentrated thought that Coffey has worked into the revised line is remarkable. By dropping the definite article he invests the flower with an added significance; by identifying this flower with 'thou' it becomes a symbol of the muse.[25] The line can be read as a parenthetical description of 'thou' or as something desired of her, namely a symbol of herself. As Dhaenens suggests: 'Il peut néanmoins dire: Rends-moi toi même, – ou plutôt: Rends-moi l'image de toi même . . .'.[26] Coffey has worked within the given syntax and the highly stylised mode of the poem to highlight the tensions that inhere in the original line, tensions that are reflected in its seemingly problematic grammar. It would be a clear breach of the rules of French grammar if 'désolé' described the current state of the speaker's heart. Yet how could his heart be 'desolated' if he possessed the flower or muse? Surely this would imply that some kind of loss or 'widowhood' was attendant on possession of the flower/ muse. It is important to note that the uncertainty of the original arises out of Nerval's use of the French imperfect which, if rendered word for word in English, would read something like, 'The flower which was pleasing so much my desolate heart'. Coffey has caught this central ambiguity wonderfully in the revised line. It is worth comparing the original and the two versions:

La fleur qui plaisait tant à mon coeur désolé,

(l. 7)

the flower which so won my heart desolated

(1975)

flower which pleased so my heart desolated,

(1997)

In the first version the flower seems to possess a positive value and 'won' clearly functions as a transitive verb with 'so' acting as an intensifier. The new version is an improvement because it enables Coffey to play on several meanings of 'pleased': if we understand it as a transitive verb, the line has a similar meaning to the first version; should we choose to understand it as an intransitive verb, however, 'desolated' flickers into life as a verb with 'flower' as its subject and 'heart' as the object. There is, of course, another reading of the line in which 'so' can be taken to mean 'also' or 'likewise' in which case the 'flower' confers both pleasure and desolation simultaneously rather than alternately. Evidently, for Nerval, those who wish to commune with the muse must pay a price – like Orpheus – and this implicates his poem in the whole question of values.[27] Coffey's translation, as J.C.C. Mays argues, draws the reader's attention to these values.[28] The fascinating thing about the translation is that the features that give it the appearance of being wooden and unwieldy – the fidelity to the original syntax, the stylised idiom with its archaisms and inversions  – enable Coffey to trace the undercurrents of thought and feeling that are there in the original. It is this deeper level of meaning that Coffey wants to explore in order to point up the values that inhere in the work and engage more fully with them.

Derek Mahon's version of the poem proceeds from a different, more conventional understanding of the the translator's craft. With its nicely maintained rhyme scheme, clear syntax and distinctly English rhythms, his version certainly succeeds in creating the impression that it is an original English poem. A dilution of meaning is inevitable and this can best be illustrated by comparing his version of the second quatrain with Coffey's.

> To the dark tomb, you who assuaged my hurt,
> Bring me Posilipo and the Tyrrhenian sea,
> The flower that comforted my desolate heart
> And the vine-leaves of the rose-wreathed balcony.[29]

The two versions complement each other but it is instructive to read how some critics regard the loss of Nerval's psychological complexity and density of thought as some kind of coup: 'Derek Mahon's versions from Nerval venture much . . . and gain thereby a lustre and smoothness missing in the original.'[30] Presumably the critic approved of Mahon's omission of Nerval's historical and mythical allusions in line 9 and his decision to substitute them with a token of antiquity. This version of the line provides a classic example of how translators domesticate foreign texts:

> Suis-je Amour ou Phébus? . . . Lusignan ou Biron?
>
> (Nerval)

> I am what childe of legend or romance?
>
> (Mahon)

Besides possessing a beauty of their own, Nerval's allusions are significant. In Mahon's version, this line could be interpreted as an expression of a crisis of identity, which it is, of course. The line must also be understood, however, as a progression to a new level of consciousness as the speaker not only recognises but *names* the oppositions that exist within himself and articulates them in two carefully balanced hemistichs. The poem will now move towards a dialectical resolution of the oppositions that these hemistichs embrace and suggest a recovery of lost unity. Exegetical texts abound with detailed analyses of the significance of these names but for the present purpose it suffices to identify the important polarities of darkness/night (Amour) and light/day (Phébus).

Coffey's first version acknowledges the significance of these names but his departure from the lineation and punctuation of the original suggests that he wished to interrogate the value and the nature of the hard won synthesis that concludes the sonnet. There is no good reason to detach the third line of the tercet from the second because taken together they constitute another reformulation of the oppositions contained in the first. The queen and the siren are also different manifestations of the same being – namely, the muse in her respective diurnal and nocturnal incarnations. More subtly, the two lines taken together echo the ambivalence of this being: she can confer blessings but she can also give rise to sterile dreams. The remaining mark of the kiss implies an intimate link, the dream implies separation and distance. There is another case for retaining the original form: out of the passivity of the first tercet – the punctuation is crucial here – necessarily arises the activity and creativity of the final one. We can only suppose that in his first version, Coffey intended to give an added prominence to the third line but he did so at the expense of disrupting the equal balance of oppositions. The dropped pronoun in the first line of the second tercet suggests that he was trying to emphasise the passage from passivity into activity but his altered lineation strongly suggests that all that follows occurs in a dream, an effect heightened by the ellipsis.

Coffey may have decided to depart from the original lineation in order to make a specific point. In *Advent II* Coffey mounts a critique on modern Western poetry in which Petrarch, Mallarmé and Nerval stand as practitioners of the cult of 'Laura false advent idol'. The entire section is filled with references to sleeping and dreaming: 'So they breathed in beauty . . . / as if dreaming sleep called back Eden awakening sad'.[31] The muse (Laura) yields 'a joy futureless', a dream from which man must awake to inevitable disappointment. The poem develops the argument that Western culture has evolved into an expression of man's desire to recover a lost paradise – 'those golden realms'– with the result that certain values have displaced other values that are necessary for the regulation of man's relationship with the world. The dynamic of Coffey's later poetry, especially the love poems, derives from his need to reconcile these conflicting sets of values. Orpheus stands as a representative figure. His music is a substitute for something lost but it induces a sleep-like state that renders him and his listeners insensible to the world. Coffey's revisions mark an acknowledgement that Nerval was fully aware of the ambivalent nature of his commitment to poetry.[32]

Coffey's careful and intensive revisions of the tercets and his deviant translations of 'soupirs' and 'cris' are important. Some will argue that 'modulating and 'inflecting' are synonyms but within the economy of a Coffey translation the decision to use one alternative rather than the other is motivated by a wish to make a specific point. It probably occured to Coffey that a more obvious translation of 'tour à tour' would have given him the extra stress to construct a line that would have scanned conveniently into six iambs: 'inflecting turn and turn about on Orpheus' lyre'. Coffey refuses such an option at this crucial stage because it would amount to a renunciation of the principles that have governed his translation thus far. A careful reading of the original line ('Modulant tour à tour sur la lyre d'Orphée') will show that Nerval's metrics are very subtle indeed and depend upon a caesura after the second 'tour'. Coffey reproduces Nerval's caesurae as they play an important function in pointing up the oppositions that lend the poem its creative tension. Had he given the above alternative the repetition of 'turn' would have given the line a strong forward momentum and the caesura would have been lost. The unfamiliarity of the phrase 'turn about' creates the necessary pause – albeit a slight one. The revisions of the last line mark a similar kind of response to the rhythm of the original. Note how Coffey converts 'soupirs' into a participle in the revised version but retains the noun form – albeit singular – of 'cris' in order to match syllable for syllable the movement and rhythm of Nerval's line:

> Les soupirs de la sainte et les cris de la fée.

> The sighing of the saint and the cry of the fay.

Coffey's preparedness to sacrifice meaning for the sake of something he considers more essential – here rhythm and syntax– is almost provocative. One thinks of the aforementioned Zukofsky translations of Catullus. Like Coffey, the Zukofskys are faithful to the lineation of the poem and their lines often contain exactly the same number of syllables as Catullus's. In the case of the Zukofsky translations a phonetic correspondence mediates between the Latin text and the English; Coffey, on the other hand, moulds his English around the armature of French syntax. What strikes one about both styles is that while they refuse to pander to the reader's desire for 'accessible meanings' they manage to throw light on the meaning of the original in a way that more conventional translations do not. Coffey's translation of line 7 of 'El Desdichado' or the opening lines of 'Le Bateau ivre' could be cited as perfect illustrations of this. Burton Hatlen has provided a very interesting analysis of the Zukofskys' translation of 'Carmen 32':

> Amabo, mea dulcis Ipsithilla,
> meae deliciae, mei lepores,
> iube ad te veniam meridiatum

> I'm a bow, my dual kiss, Ipsithilla,
> my daily key, eye, my eye's little leap-horse,
> you bid me to 'when,' I'm your meridian.

The auditory correspondence is indisputable but at first sight it would appear that the translation is meaningless. Yet in their quest for a homo-phonic translation the Zukofskys have found another way to render the earthy humour and sense of the original. Hatlen gives some very good reasons why 'I'm a bow' picks up meanings which are latent in Catullus's 'Amabo'.[33] What Lawrence Venuti writes about the Zufosky translations could equally apply to Coffey's: 'The opacity of the language is due, however, not to the absence of meaning, but to the release of multiple meanings specific to English.'[34] The two methods may focus on different aspects of the text but their underlying principles are very similar.

A brief comparison of Coffey's and Robin Blaser's versions of 'Vers dorés', the last sonnet in the sequence, will illustrate what I mean when I argue that Coffey's mode of engagement is dialogic rather that dialectical.

Nerval's sonnet opens rhetorically. The first quatrain acknowledges man's special place in the universe but it also reprimands him for pursuing an exclusively homocentric vision that alienates him from the universe of which he is an integral part.

> Homme, libre penseur! te crois-tu seul pensant
> Dans ce monde où la vie éclate en toute chose?
> Des forces que tu tiens ta liberté dispose,
> Mais de tous tes conseils l'univers est absent.[35]

The sentiments expressed here are not unlike those expressed in parts of *Advent*, although, unlike Nerval, Coffey does not argue for a pantheistic vision of the universe. His version tracks the shifting tonalities of the quatrain: the initial address is undercut by a rhetorical question; the relative praise and acknowledgement of line 3 is then cast in an ironic light by the unequivocal condemnation of line 4:

> Man, free thinker! do you believe you only
> think in this world where life bursts out of each thing?
> Of powers in your grasp your freedom disposes
> but from all your plans the universe is absent.[36]

The sense of line 3 of the poem is suggested in Coffey's version, yet it is interesting to note that in the line that most closely matches Nerval's syntax he makes another meaning available. Nerval's argument implicates man's rational faculties, his ability to conceive of a plan and implement it. Coffey allows this, but he qualifies Nerval's assumptions by playing on two senses of 'dispose of' in order to highlight the ambivalence of man's freedom. Man can choose to use his powers in a rational way but he is also free to use them wastefully. *Advent VIII* meditates on the gift of freedom and identifies it as the crux of human morality: it 'saves from bondage/ is gift. . . . / is height of power . . .'. Yet this 'gift' also includes the 'freedom to choose unending night'.[37] Nerval's pantheism and his valorisation of human freedom are allowed to stand, but Coffey manages to imply other values, specifically Christian ones, against which Nerval's are tested. [38]

Robin Blaser's approach to translation is different from Coffey's because he wishes to present free-standing poems. Coffey, on the other hand, wishes to present free-standing translations. The distinction is important because I do not believe that Coffey wished to present a finished work that would stand independently of the poem; instead, he endeavours to present an exploded view of the original poem in a way that is obviously dependent on its forms and he tests the values and assumptions that those forms embrace.

Blaser was interested not so much in catching the psychological accuracy of perception in the language of his poems; rather, the poem had to comprehend the 'processional aspect' of the world: 'The body hears the world, and the power of the earth over the body . . . is in terms of rhythms, meters, phrasing, picked up . . .'.[39] As we shall see, Blaser brings his own thinking to bear on 'Vers dorés', the final sonnet in the sequence and one that raises issues that are fundamental for him – and Coffey – in a very creative way. His translation retains Nerval's central opposition of rational man and the universe but Blaser looks at this opposition from a different perspective. Now man's security is contingent upon factors beyond his control; moreover, he lives in the shadow of his mortality– he is defined as 'free of the dead'. While he may be blessed with the capacity to think, man's rational faculties are delimited by 'what can be thought' and this does not include access to the hidden systems of a world 'where it all coheres'. Unlike Coffey, who, as we have seen, is interested in highlighting and testing the values that inform Nerval's rhetoric, Blaser sheds the rhetorical flourishes of the original poem. There is no sense of condemnation. He scales down and carefully qualifies any claim that can be made for man's pre-eminence.

> free of the dead,
> what *can* be thought
> *seems* to be yours in this world
> where it all coheres
> free to spend *some* powers
> but the universe is absent
> from all your plans[40]

> [The italics are mine; the underlining is the author's]

In this context, Nerval's 'Mais de tous tes conseils l'univers est absent' is strangely present but the line is transposed into an utterly different, more ironic tonality. In Blaser's translation the universe is indeed absent from man's projects not because it is excluded from man's homocentric vision but because the universe is finally unknowable.

His translation of the second quatrain and the first tercet, which I cite below with the corresponding passage from the original, illustrates what he means when he writes that his poems attempt to 'pick up' the 'processional aspect of the world'.

Respecte dans la bête un esprit agissant:
Chaque fleur est une âme à la nature éclose;
Un mystère d'amour dans le métal repose;
"Tout est sensible!" Et tout sur ton être est puissant.

Crains, dans le mur aveugle, un regard qui t'épie:
A la matière même un verbe est attaché. . .
Ne la fais pas servir à quelque usage impie![41]

take the ghost stirring
in an animal      each
flower,      a piece of light
scattering      love's mystery
asleep in metal alive
the coherence takes power
over you

in the blind wall,      you fear
the blindness which sees you
even to matter,      put to
true and false uses,
a word is tied

Again, the substance of the original poem is present but it is radically transformed. While Coffey does not alter the lineation of the poem and separates the animal, vegetative and mineral realms by retaining Nerval's end-stops, Blaser uses enjambment to suggest the integrity or *coherence* of the world and the interdependence of all its elements. The relationship between smaller rhythmic units is stengthened by internal rhyme, assonance and alliteration while the enjambment in the third paragraph is particularly significant: 'you fear/ the blindness which sees you/ even to matter . . .'.

Unlike Blaser who brings his own concerns to bear on Nerval's poem in a way that necessarily involves radical changes to its form and shape, Coffey's reponse is determined by specific events in the poem. Blaser's mode is dialectical. In many ways he includes and transcends or exceeds the original poem, much like a composer presenting variations on a given theme: 'In my view, these translations required that I become Nerval and yet remain my own poet.'[42] Coffey's mode is dialogic or, to extend the musical analogy, polyphonic: his translation moves with the poem while simultaneously suggesting other meanings that comment on the values inherent in the poem. If he were to exceed the original radically in the way that Blaser does, Coffey would negate the value of his own critique. It is this unique kind of engagement that makes Coffey's translation of Mallarmé's poetry so remarkable.

\*      \*      \*

In 1965 the Dolmen Press published Coffey's version of Mallarmé's masterwork, *Un Coup de dés jamais n'abolira le hasard*, a poem which presents the translator with a unique challenge. The poem relies so heavily on orthographic, homonymic and polysemic elements specific to French that some commentators have pronounced it to be untranslatable.[43] Few texts possess as many simultaneous possibilities of conjunction or so flatly deny a consecutive, linear reading as Mallarmé's last work. The use of space is unprecedented. Normally assigned an organising function in poetic texts, space now distracts the reader by denying clear rational patterns. Small fragments of language that barely make any sense when read in isolation are surrounded by white blanks. How, for example, does one translate a word that is so detached that it hardly seems to function as a signifier, like the isolated 'par' on opening 3? Or how does one translate the many strands of thought that run concurrently through the poem so that they will interact meaningfully?

Again, musical analogies help to appreciate the difficulty of translating this incredibly complex text. It resembles a huge orchestral work and at times it is so densely textured that it is almost impossible to appreciate everything that is going on at any single moment in its unfolding. Any translation of such a work inevitably results in some thinning out of its texture, and those handicapped by a lack of French cannot experience the full symphonic complexity of the poem.

Brian Coffey adopts the strategy of providing something akin to a reduced piano score. The main lines of thought are carefully preserved; he selects motifs that can be rendered contrapuntally in English such as the punning on words associated with gaming or the act of writing. While Coffey continually endeavours to render something of the depth and subtlety of Mallarmé's thinking, his translation does not focus on rendering the conceptual content alone. The rhythms of the original are carefully attended to so that the reader follows the movement of Mallarmé's French. The poem often features particular groupings of words from different associative fields and the logic of their association is often so tenuous that the reader is obliged to ponder the meaning of the sound patterns that lend the grouping a more obvious cogency. By rendering this tension between phonetic and syntactic patterns, Coffey recreates those conditions that enable the reader of the original poem to engage creatively with its different modes of signification.

The layout and typography of *Un Coup de dés*, complete with 11 character styles and double-page format, is reproduced faithfully with one very important exception, to which I shall return later (see p. 79).[44] The success of Coffey's translation in this respect owed much to the improved presswork of the Dolmen Press. Its founder, Liam Miller, was a perfectionist and he used his small profits to procure new founts and better materials for his print shop. Given these resources one might suppose that reproducing the visual aspect of the original poem would be the least of the translator's problems. Such is the peculiar nature of *Un Coup de dés*, however, that the translator must find a way of replicating the physical layout of the text as accurately as possible without losing the meaning of the poem. It is worth remembering that Mallarmé's emendations to the Lahure proof are exact down to one-sixteenth of an inch; one correction requests that a particular word be shifted forward so that the ends of words in the group to which it belongs form a straight oblique line. Consider then the dilemma facing the translator who is confronted with this particular fragment from opening 6.

*Une insinuation        simple . . .*

                              *le mystère*
                                    *précipité*
                                          *hurlé*
                                          . . .

                                                    COMME SI[45]

Henry Weinfield privileges the visual aspect of this passage and maintains the angle through which the words '*le mystère/ précipité/ hurlé*' descend the page by placing each successive word beneath the exact point at which the previous word ended, much as Mallarmé intended.

*An insinuation        simple . . . .*

                              *the mystery*
                                    *hurled*
                                          *howled*
                                          . . .

                                                    AS IF[46]

One can easily appreciate the visual correspondence between the translation and the poem. The particular sense that Mallarmé assigns to 'précipité', however, which evokes the imagined fall of the secret ('*insinuation*') down into the realm of historical time, is hardly evoked by 'hurled'. Coffey's more accurate translation of the French participles involves the addition of prepositions. Yet in order to prevent the smaller italicised print from encroaching on the right-hand space reserved for the second '*AS IF*' Coffey must place the participles several spaces to the left:

*An insinuation          merely . . .*
                    *the mystery*
                        *flung down*
                            *howled out*
                        . . .


                                            *AS IF*[47]


While it could be argued that such slight alterations hardly matter in a translation, the question of placement is in fact the central problem of rendering this unique work. For example, the translation of the title phrase, out of which the rest of the poem ramifies like branches from a central trunk, will determine the thrust and ultimately the degree of success of the whole enterprise. The sense, sound and rhythm of the original phrase have to be attended to of course, but the translator is translating more than an individual fragment of language: he is attempting to dismantle and re-structure what Gardner Davies calls 'l'épine dorsale intellectuelle et syntactique du poème.'[48] Before examining the broader implications of rendering this title phrase, I want to briefly examine Coffey's translation of it as an isolated fragment of language and compare it with Weinfield's. Here is the original phrase as it was given on the title page of the Lahure proof which Mallarmé had approved – note the capitals:

          *Un coup de Dés jamais n'abolira le Hasard.*

Virginia La Charité points out that the upper case letters indicate emphasis and word-value and that '*Dés*' and '*Hasard*' receive maximum reader attention and interest.[49] Coffey gives these words their due prominence by placing their corresponding terms in English at the beginning and the end of the title phrase: 'Dice Thrown Never Will Annul Chance'.

In the original title phrase Mallarmé reverses the normal word order of the French by placing 'jamais' before 'n'abolira'. Coffey renders this with an inversion that some might consider ungainly: '. . .Never Will Annul. . .'. This apparent clumsiness can be construed as a very skilful piece of translation for reasons I shall discuss later (see p. 73). The verb 'Annul' renders better the sense of Mallarmé's 'Abolir'. Like the English 'abolish', the French verb was usually said of institutions or customs as in 'abolir une loi, une coutume'. According to the Larousse Dictionary, however, 'abolir' also has a very specific sense in literary discourse, its nearest synonyms being 'anéantir' or 'détruire'.[50] Now this sense of 'abolir' is closely matched by 'annul' for which the OED gives as its first definition 'to reduce to nothing, annihilate, to put out of existence'. [51]

Mallarmé sought to increase the truth value of his poem by embedding it in self-negation. In an obvious reference to Mallarmé in *Advent II* Coffey uses the phrase 'inverted hybris' to describe an aesthetic that founds its claim to truth upon self-negation (*PV* 121). Coffey incorporates this important element of Mallarmé's thinking into his translation in a way which suggests that the logic that informs *Un Coup de dés* can be turned back on itself and his arrangement of the constituent parts of the proposition across the poem is calculated to amplify its latent positive element. He does not distort the sense of the phrase, which, when dispersed throughout the text, becomes inherently unstable anyway. Coffey, then, sets out to investigate the hidden possibilities of a poem which seeks to negate all, yet is felt to be continually flirting with positive meaning.

In his commentary to *Un Coup de dés*, Weinfield notes that 'jamais' can mean both 'never' and 'ever' and that the central phrase wavers between positive and negative meaning as it unfolds through the poem. He goes on to argue that this is an effect 'that English is unable to capture, since it is obliged to indicate the negative immediately'.[52] Weinfield's translation of the title phrase – 'A Throw Of The Dice Will Never Abolish Chance' – and his disposal of its constituent parts across the poem are determined by this early admission of defeat. Coffey, on the other hand, reconstitutes the wavering effect of the original title phrase by an inversion of the normal word order which generates an oscillation between the negative and positive terms **NEVER** and **WILL**.

Needless to say, the precise order of the words is crucial for several reasons. Coffey needs a form that not only expresses the complexity of the original phrase but that will interact effectively with the rest of the poem so that multiple meanings – meanings that already exist in the poem and other new meanings that challenge Mallarmé's – can be released. Consequently, neither **DICE THROWN/ WILL/ NEVER ANNUL/ CHANCE** nor **DICE THROWN/ WILL NEVER/ ANNUL/ CHANCE** would serve either end. While Mallarmé's **N'ABOLIRA** stands monolithically at the bottom right hand corner of opening 5, confirming the negative sense of the proposition to which it belongs and sealing off the positive value latent in **JAMAIS,** Coffey's **WILL ANNUL** continues the sense of the proposition but opens up new possibilities of positive meaning by linking an auxiliary which expresses positive intent with the infinitive. The experience of reading this passage is highly unusual. Because of the earlier inversion the object of the verb (**CHANCE**) comes more readily to mind than its subject and the alternative possibilty of the existence of a 'subject' or an agency capable of bestowing order and annulling chance is fleetingly glimpsed. Coffey's translation of the phrase and his disposal of it across the text – **DICE THROWN/**

**NEVER/ WILL ANNUL/ CHANCE** – makes for a translation that bristles with meaning.[53]

Coffey, as I have said, does not wilfully distort the general sense of the main idea, but the way he casts its elements in the new language certainly means that the values bound up in it are put to the proof; to adapt a passage from one of Coffey's own poems, these values face a testing against others based on different grounds. Note how the positive quality of **WILL ANNUL (CHANCE)** is reinforced by the fact that it appears to connect up with a sequence of similar verb forms which descend opening 5:

> born
> of play
>
> the sea via the old one trying or the old one against the sea
>               a useless chance
>
>                                         Betrothals
> of which
>         the illusory veil spun again their hauntingness
>         like the ghost of a geste
>                         will totter
>                         will collapse
>
>                 madness                    **WILL ANNUL**
>
>                                         (*DT* O.5)

By following the clear diagonal that connects 'Betrothals' to **WILL ANNUL (CHANCE)** the reader notices another intersection that creates positive meanings not available in the original. New negative meanings are simultaneously suggested by the obvious references to matrimony, 'Betrothals' and 'annul'.

The excerpt cited above merits some attention. The corresponding passage in the original poem is exceedingly complex and Coffey deploys every device at his disposal to realise its density in his translation. The passage needs to be put into its context. This opening (5) continues the narrative commenced at the top of the previous opening which tells of the demise of the Master of a sunken vessel. Here we must remember the phrase on opening 2, WHEN EVEN INDEED CAST IN CIRCUMSTANCES OF ETERNITY. All that follows, then, must be understood as a purely hypothetical case. The sinking Master hesitates to throw the dice, which in any event will be a futile gesture. A throw of the dice may affirm chance; however, if the throw were to negate chance by resulting in the anticipated number, it would ultimately be a number determined by chance. The narrative illustrates the central argument of the poem: affirmation and negation of chance are finally equivalent. Later, Mallarmé will allow one posssible exception to this general rule: the hypothetical dice throw (or poem) that acknowledges its own absurdity and proceeds in the knowledge that chance can never be annuled contains its own criticism and by negating negation it may suppress chance.

The alternatives facing the Master both lead to the same conclusion. Like *Hamlet*, hesitation or procrastination is the creative principle of *Un Coup de dés*. The hesitation of the Master is mirrored in the continual interruptions – often themselves interrupted – illustrations and qualifications that constitute the poem. Both alternatives are held in equal suspension and Mallarmé realises this hesitation at the level of form. It is instructive to compare the first lines of the passage cited above to the corresponding passage in the original to see how closely Coffey matches it.

> né
> d'un ébat
>
> la mer par l'aïeul tentant ou l'aïeul contre la mer
> une chance oiseuse
>
> (CD O.5)

It is worth noting that Mallarmé had revised an earlier version of the third line – 'la mer tentant par l'aïeul ou lui contre la mer'– in order to realise through syntax a symmetry which would exemplify the spirit of 'symphonic equation' which informs the whole poem.[54] Coffey's literal translation has far-reaching benefits. By referring back to the previous opening the reader can 'unpack' the two distinct alternatives folded into this line. The 'old one' (the Master) will either refuse 'to play/ . . .*in the name of the waves*' (*DT* O.4) and resist the sea long enough to throw the dice, in which case he will be 'trying . . . against the sea/ a useless chance' (*DT* O.5). Alternatively, he might consent to 'play/ . . . *in the name of the waves*' and allow himself to drown without throwing the dice, in which case 'the sea via the old one' tries its chance.[55] By translating 'ébat' as 'play' rather than 'frolics' Coffey consolidates a thread of thought that intermittently alludes to gambling by focusing his puns more specifically on card-playing: he renders Mallarmé's 'jouer/. . . la partie' as 'play/ . . ./ the hand' (*DT* O.4). The issue of this inevitable union or 'conjunction with probability' will be 'born /of play'; chance will determine the outcome, regardless of the decision taken by the Master.[56]

I have emphasised the point that this passage must be understood as a narrative of an event which has not yet taken place because many translators have failed to appreciate the role this fiction plays within the overall scheme of the poem. Weinfield's translation, for example, is seriously flawed by his inaccurate translation of Mallarmé's 'Fiançailles' as 'Nuptials' which suggests that he has mistaken this union of the

Master and the sea as something that has already taken place. It is vital to the life of the poem and to the life of any subsequent translation that this union be repeatedly postponed.[57] Closure is approached asymptotically, the final 'coup' of the poem being that it concludes by suggesting an ultimate moment without relating an achieved act. Coffey's 'Betrothals' is consistent with the meaning of the entire narrative: the dice is still 'clenched' above the surface of the sea, 'beyond the useless head' of the Master (DT O.5).

The next lines contain a classic example of Coffey's usage of deviant translation. Both Douglas Sealy and Parkman Howe singled out this passage for criticism, the latter suggesting that Coffey's translation of Mallarmé's 'le fantôme d'un geste' was 'overly literal'.[58] It is worth quoting the original passage and looking again at Coffey's translation of it:

                                        Fiançailles
        dont
                le voile d'illusion rejailli leur hantise
                ainsi que le fantôme d'un geste

                                        (CD O.5)


                                        Betrothals
        of which
                the illusory veil spun again their hauntingness
                like the ghost of a geste

                                        (DT O.5)

As Gardner Davies rightly argues, 'the veil' of the fiancée symbolises the raised arm or hesitation of the Master.[59] Yet in the context of the unfolding drama we know that any hesitation is ultimately pointless because the alternatives will both lead to the same end. Coffey renders the complicated sense of the original which Weinfield translates as 'the veil of illusion sprung up against their haunting' (p. 132). Coffey's translation makes this meaning available by using 'again' in its archaic sense, as 'in resistance to' or 'against'. The passage takes on many of the qualities that Jacques Le Cercle observed in his examination of alternative models of translation; Coffey's text becomes a 'locus for diachrony-within-synchrony, the place of inscription for past and present linguistic conjunctures.'[60] The bridal veil, then, is 'spun' against the Master's final union with the sea. Like the hand held above the waves, the veil temporarily forestalls the inevitable union and it signifies an act that has not yet been accomplished; but in another way – like the hand that will succumb to the waves and relax its grip on the dice thus unleashing chance – the veil also foretells or announces the union 'again'. Coffey's translation conveys this additional sense. Chance has been spun into the veil so that any gesture, dice-throw or poem that attempts to suppress chance is actually contaminated from within by the very thing it attempts to annul: it 'will totter/ will collapse', inevitably.

Poetry is exceptional only in so far as it acknowledges the all-pervasive power of chance. The new self-negating poem that Mallarmé endeavoured to write affirms its own precipitous existence and, by comparison with earlier genres, it will seem 'like the ghost of a geste' because unlike the literary genre to which it alludes – the 'geste' –, his poem does not record any performed 'act'. Coffey notes Mallarmé's play on 'tome' in 'le fantôme d'un geste' but he relocates the covert reference to writing by retaining 'geste'– a word listed in English dictionaries.[61] Weinfield (p. 132) and Hartley (p. 221) lose the self-reflexive significance of the line by translating it as 'like the ghost of a gesture'.[62]

This destined 'conjunction with probability' has become an obsession ('hantise'), one that haunts the poem as it does the Master. No obstacle can be placed against an imminent destiny, yet when considered from the perspective of the present, this truth – that every result will be determined solely by the operation of chance – can only exist as a notion in the mind of the Master or in the text of the poem. 'Hauntingness', a nonce word, captures the essence of this mystery superbly: it does not exist as a word in the language of the text; however, it does exist as word on the page and the reader can guess at its intended meaning.

This passage of *Dice Thrown* is acutely self-reflexive and it pulls the reader up short as the translator signals his presence in a very manifest way. In his introduction to *Dice Thrown* Coffey reminds the reader that the text s/he is about to read is only 'an approximation to a *calk* [tracing]' of Mallarmé's poem. The wording of the phrase is significant for it suggests that what we are about to read is at several removes from the original work. It is almost impossible to avoid feeling that in the passage under consideration Coffey, like Mallarmé, is also playing on the sense of 'geste' as a literary genre so that the line 'like the ghost of a geste' intentionally echoes the proviso contained in the introduction. One may ask why Coffey asserts his visibility at this particular point in his translation. After all, this is a culminating moment within the scheme of *Un Coup de dés* because it ends the fiction that illustrates the central argument of the poem and brings all its strands of thought together so that they converge in one moment of absolute negation.

In the opening just discussed Coffey inscribes his convictions via his reconstruction of the main stem or spine of *Un Coup de dés* and by the way this carefully crafted title phrase interacts with smaller print to amplify positive meanings latent in the original poem. I want to consider his translation of opening 9 for it is here that Coffey openly declares his own beliefs. This opening contains another culminating passage, one which finally reveals the absurdity of the Master's hesitation. The revelation is all the more overwhelming because several different strands of thought converge and fuse with the typography to produce another powerful synthesis. It combines the conjunction *SI* (8 point italics in upper-case) on opening 8 with the hypothetical proposition which it introduces on opening 9, *C'ÉTAIT LE NOMBRE CE SERAIT* (12 point bold upper-case). The proposition is completed by **LE HASARD** (22 point upper-case roman), which also functions as the object of **N'ABOLIRA** and completes the long parenthetical strand which commenced with THE MASTER.

Coffey reproduces the lettering and translates the proposition faithfully: *IF/ IT WAS THE NUMBER IT WOULD BE/ CHANCE*. He takes as his point of resistance the series of speculative phrases that examine this hypothetical number under its different aspects: EXISTÂT-IL/ COMMENÇÂT-IL ET CESSÂT-IL/ SE CHIFFRÂT-IL/ ILLUMINÂT-IL. Properly translated into English, these imperfect-subjunctive phrases would read WERE IT TO EXIST/ WERE IT TO BEGIN . . . .[63] The sequencing of these phrases is significant: the text has now brought the reader so deeply into into the realm of hypothesis that the material existence of this number can only be imagined and, what is more, even if it did exist in the material world its operation would be determined solely by chance. An appreciation of what Mallarmé means by *LE NOMBRE* is necessary if we are to understand what motivates Coffey's resistance to Mallarmé's argument. Firstly, it represents an actual number, the result of the ideal dice throw and were it to exist the Master would be delivered. In so far as the poem can be understood as an allegory, *LE NOMBRE* also possesses an epistemological and metaphysical significance: its existence guarantees that man's experience of the world can be organised into coherent and truthful structures. Orthographically, (N)OMBRE negates shadow and chaos, and illuminates an otherwise dark world; by the same token it also 'contains' the forces it seeks to suppress, much like the Master's fist clenched above the waves.

It is this passage of *Un Coup de dés* in particular that cuts right against Coffey's most fundamental principles. On purely philosophical grounds Coffey would object that the sciences do constitute knowledge of the physical world, as this extract from a long review article he wrote for *The Modern Schoolman* shows:

> The thesis of the degrees of intellective abstraction which may be found in the works of St Thomas does provide a basis for the solution of the problem of the applicability of mathematical propositions to the world of existent things.

Towards the end of the article he writes: 'Science now provides a powerful suasion towards the truths of religion.'[64]

Returning to *Dice Thrown*, we find that Coffey has translated the aforementioned series of phrases begining with 'EXISTÂT-IL' as follows: (*THE NUMBER*) MIGHT IT EXIST/ MIGHT IT BEGIN AND MIGHT IT END/ MIGHT IT BE COUNTED/ MIGHT IT ILLUMINE (O.9). Hypothetical propositions expressed through subjunctive verb forms have now mutated into questions of fact, albeit tentatively put. The reader is invited to consider, or rather he is reminded of, the possibility that the 'number' might in fact exist 'otherwise than hallucination of scattered spray' (O.9), and that the 'number' might illumine **CHANCE**. It is no error then that this opening should feature the only significant departure from the layout of the original poem. In *Un Coup dés*, the series of phrases just discussed are distributed at regularly spaced intervals down the right hand side of the page so that the first and last phrases are almost equidistant from *LE NOMBRE* and **LE HASARD** respectively. Virginia La Charité writes that 'the imperfect subjunctive verb forms are reinforced by their spatial suspension, literally set aside, having no analogue'.[65] In *Dice Thrown* these forms are physically lifted out of the field of force surrounding **CHANCE**; now clustered into a cohesive unit around *THE NUMBER*, they suggest that this concept may indeed possess an 'analogue' in the material world (see illustrations). This is an important gesture, at once expressive of Coffey's trust in the existence of truths which are accessible by virtue of those faculties bestowed on man by God – a sense conveyed by a choice of verb form that could also express aspiration – and of his need to signify his resistance to the far-reaching implications of Mallarmé's proposition. Reason and intelligence were for Coffey genuine and sufficient causes of true knowledge within the natural order.

Coffey weaves his convictions into the fabric of the next opening too by picking up and developing meanings latent in the poem. In a manner reminiscent of his Nerval versions, Coffey again displays a remarkable knack for signifying his commitments through close engagement with the original text. No other translator of *Un Coup de dés* has taken account of the strange coinage in this passage:

RIEN

    de la mémorable crise
      ou se fût
        l'évènement    accompli en vue de tout résultat nul
                                    humain

            N'AURA EU LIEU
            une élévation ordinaire verse l'absence

                    QUE LE LIEU
           inferieure clapotis quelconque comme . . .

                      (CD O.10)

The portmanteau word 'l'évènement' is an obvious cross between 'l'évenement' ('event') and 'l'avènement' ('advent') – the grave accent on the second *e* was not a misprint as Mallarmé's handwritten emendations in the Lahure proof clearly show. Not only does Coffey catch the double significance of this word but he also renders the reflexive form 'se fût accompli', unlike Weinfield and Hartley. No discussion of this passage could omit some mention of the wonderful technique it displays. In the lower lines of this passage, rhythm and sound patterning combine to create a marvellous seascape for the ear.[66]

NOTHING

    of the memorable crisis
      or might have
        the event    come about of itself in view of every result nul
                                      human

            WILL HAVE TAKEN PLACE
            an everyday uplifting pours out absence

                    BUT PLACE
    commonplace plashing below of waves as for dispersing . . .

                    (DT O.10)

    Coffey captures much of the original sense of lines 2–5 which might be paraphrased thus: 'bearing in mind that the Master – or man – will have disappeared, the dice throw, were it to come about, would have no consequence even when every possible result is taken into account'. Yet the passage is so constructed as to suggest simultaneously the theoretical possibility that an event or dice throw might have occurred the cause of which was other than human. Line 4 of the excerpt certainly permits a construction like, 'might the event have come about of itself'. The translation of 'une élévation ordinaire verse l'absence' is deeply ambiguous as it expresses two mutually contradictory meanings. 'To pour out absence' can mean 'to void' or 'empty out', which conveys the sense of 'verse'; conversely, it can mean 'to fill with presence' and I would suggest that the fragment 'an ordinary elevation pours out absence' is intended to echo Isaiah 53:12 and Joel 2:28, two passages which foretell, respectively, the Advent of Christ and the descent of the Holy Spirit upon the Apostles.[67] These traces of positive value exist like watermarks in *Dice Thrown*: they are visible when looked for and they authenticate the translation as an act of total engagement, Coffey's values simultaneously testing, and being tested by, Mallarmé's.

It must be emphasised that Coffey was deeply appreciative of Mallarmé's poetry. Indeed he wrote that Mallarmé 'went further than any other in exploring the nature of poetry, and attempting to say what it is and how to make it'.[68] Coffey's translations, in turn, go further than any other in rendering in English those qualities that made Mallarmé such a special poet and in this respect they are a testament of the translator's esteem. The fundamental difference between their respective aesthetics originates in their differing conceptions of the relationship between poetry and the world of things. Poet and critic Yves Bonnefoy argues that, for Mallarmé, disappointment invariably follows perception because such is the nature of our engagement with the world that we experience only a potential beauty rather than a beauty that is actual and fully realised. Mallarmé projects all his hopes into words 'as they enable that which we conceive, but which fails to exist effectively, to re-form itself'. Nature, 'deprived of itself in empirical existence', comes into its own for the first time through verse.[69] Anyone who has read *Advent* will know that Coffey reverses this formulation of the relationship between the world and the word. As Coffey would have it, the existence of beauty owes nothing to man or to the linguistic constructions he may impose upon it; beauty exists in the physical world and not in the unworldly realm signified by the frozen swan of 'Le vierge, le vivace et le bel aujourd'hui . . .'.[70]

In order to make his point, Coffey's translation concentrates the allegorical significance of his translation on the act of writing: the verb 'cast' on opening 2 is perfectly appropriate to dicing, but it can also be said of a pen, as in 'to shed ink'; 'calculs' on opening 4 is rendered as 'cypherings' which denotes the performance of an arithmetical calculation but is more commonly used to signify a form of secret writing; in the same opening Coffey plays on several meanings of 'pens' by translating 'du secret qu'il détient' as 'from the secret it *pens*'.[71]

Readers familiar with *Un Coup de dés* will know that in the final opening Mallarmé attempts an analogical synthesis of the contingent

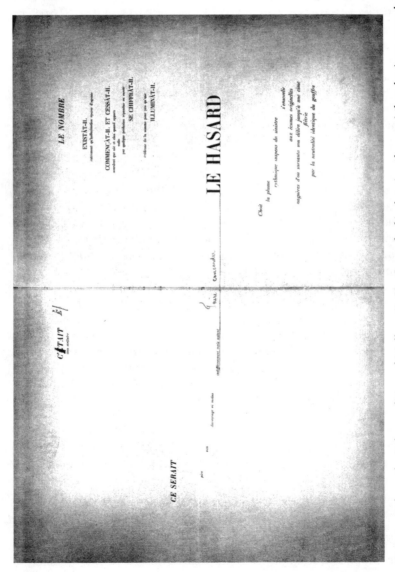

Opening 9 from the Lahure edition of Mallarmé's *Un Coup de dés* showing the poet's handwritten emendations. Mallarmé was very specific about the placement of words in this text. On this opening he instructs the typesetter to align the bottoms of 'autant' and 'LE HASARD'.

*THE NUMBER*
MIGHT IT EXIST
*otherwise than hallucination of scattered spray*
MIGHT IT BEGIN AND MIGHT IT END
*at last*
*welling up as denied and bounded on show*
*in some outpouring rarely spread*
MIGHT IT BE COUNTED

*evidence of a tot of the sum however little one*
MIGHT IT ILLUMINE

# CHANCE

*Drops*
*the quill*
*rhythmical impending of defeat*
*to bury itself*
*in the original spray*
*whence but lately whose frenzy sprang as far as a peak*
*blasted*
*by the identical neutrality of the gulf*

*IT WAS*
*born of stars*

*IT WOULD BE*
*worse*
*nor*
*more nor less*
*indifferently but as much*

Opening 9 from *Dice Thrown Never Will Annul Chance*, Coffey's version of *Un Coup de dés*. The visual layout of Coffey's text closely matches that of the original poem. This opening is the exception, however. Note how Coffey arranges his series of speculative questions into a cluster around *THE NUMBER* and distances them from **CHANCE**.

human act of the dice-throw, which may or may not have taken place, and the ideal dice throw of a constellation numbered 'sur quelque surface vacante et supérieure'. It is by way of this synthesis that Mallarmé hopes to contain chance and effect a glimpse of the fundamental truth of the universe. Coffey's translation of the final lines of the poem is a triumph. The sound of real dice clattering over a surface is caught superbly: 'the shock successive/ starwise/ of a total count in the making'. His translation of the participles that make up the handle of the Little Dipper capture the original rhythm and sense. By giving 'musing' for Mallarmé's 'méditant' and translating the final short phrase that ends the poem ('Toute Pensée émet un Coup de Dés') as 'All Thought utters Dice Thrown', Coffey consolidates the close identification of the poem and the dice throw – so much so, in fact, that by the time we reach the final stages of the translation there is an increased sense that the subject of the text we have been reading is not just the dice-throw but all poetry in general and Mallarmé's poem in particular.

> waking
> > doubting
> > > rolling
> > > > shining and musing
>
> > > before halting
> > at some latest point which crowns it
>
> > All Thought utters Dice Thrown
> > > > > (*DT* O.11)

The oddness of Coffey's translation of the the penultimate line is best illustrated by comparing it with Weinfield's and Hartley's.[72]

> > > avant de s'arrêter
> > à quelque point dernier qui le sacre
> > > > > (*CD* O.11)

> > > before coming to a halt
> > at some terminus that sanctifies it
> > > > > (Weinfield, p. 145)

> > before stopping/at some final point which consecrates it
> > > > > (Hartley, p. 233)

In *Advent II* Coffey expresses serious misgivings about Mallarmé's claim that only poetry could convey an absolute truth especially when that 'truth' posited nothingness as the source and end of all: 'Choice made on fragile ground one wooed despair/ ensorcelled took Naught as Source of All hybris positive' (*PV* 121).[73] In a strangely Mallarméan way then, Coffey increases the truth value of his translation by implying that no poetic act, however subtle its strategies, can ever amount to an expression of ultimate truth. Apart from suggesting that no single dice throw or poem can arrive at a 'terminus' or 'final point', it would have gone against Coffey's principles to confer upon any poem the type of value that words like 'sanctify' or 'consecrate' seem to claim for it. Strictly speaking the verb 'to crown' is as correct a translation of 'sacrer' as the corresponding verbs given by Weinfield and Hartley, while 'dernier' can also mean 'the most recent' or 'latest' in a continuing series.

This last opening provides another important qualification. Coffey translates the fragment at the top of the spread EXCEPTÉ/ à l'altitude' as 'EXCEPTED/ at the summit' whereas Weinfield gives 'EXCEPT/ on high'. At each of these critical moments then, Coffey deflects from the meaning of the original by restricting the scope of his translation to the realm of human experience. The reader is prepared for these departures by the provocative literalism 'EXCEPTED' which does convey – albeit obliquely – the intended sense of 'EXCEPTÉ'. This awkward literalism opens up a critical distance between the translation and the poem so that the poem is understood as the subject of the translation.[74]

Coffey employs other forms of literalism throughout *Dice Thrown* and the reader must be alert to their possible significance. On opening 8, Coffey juxtaposes a close word-for-word rendering and a deviant translation in order to create new possibilities of meaning, much as he does in the final stanza of 'The Joy-Mad Ship'. He translates Mallarmé's '*La lucide et seigneuriale aigrette de vertige/ au front invisible . . .*' as '*The lucid and lordly aigrette of vastness/ invisible on the brow. . .*'. Most translators would give 'crest' for 'aigrette' and few would dare substitute 'vastness' for 'vertigo'. Coffey has retained 'aigrette', however, because in both languages the word denotes 'crest' but more significantly it also denotes the white heron, a traditional symbol of Christ on the Mount of Olives – the Lord of 'vastness'.[75]

Before dismissing this as a fanciful interpretation the reader should examine Coffey's translation of the passage immediately above it. Mallarmé's '*soucieux/ expiatoire et pubère*' is given as '*under the weather/ scapegoat pubescent*'. The translation of the first adjective is obviously a cunning syllable-for-syllable rendering of the original word which nicely captures Mallarmé's pun on '*sous cieux*'. His translation of '*expiatoire*' is less obvious but it does anticipate the less obvious symbolism of '*aigrette*'. 'Scapegoat' was a coinage invented to translate the sacrificial goat which was laden with the sins of the Israelites and sent into the desert to be

destroyed in a ritual of atonement. Christian exegetes commonly understand the 'scapegoat' as a symbolic prefiguration of Christ's sacrifice.
Coffey then lends emphasis to one element in the cluster of references
embedded in the phrase '*expiatoire et pubère*' which, according to Robert
G. Cohn,  invokes the notion of the poet-as-Christ, a sacrificial figure
who performs the Passion of 'Catholicisme'.[76]

Many will object to Coffey's highly personal translation of *Un Coup
de dés* on the grounds that he is wilfully distorting the sense intended by
Mallarmé. Such an argument is, of course, predicated on a definition of
the translator's task that is no longer tenable now that translation studies
has openly acknowledged that every translation is *ipso facto* an interpretation. No poet or translator was more aware of the fluid and shifting
nature of language than Brian Coffey. *Un Coup de dés* is a unique poem,
as pure an expression of a highly developed aesthetic as one is likely to
encounter. Coffey could appreciate it as such without feeling obliged to
endorse the values that informed it. He uses translation to do a job that
only translation can do: he moves with the poem yet maintains a critical
distance at all times; his manner of working within the forms of the
poem enables him to mount his own specifically directed critique.

The nature of Coffey's engagement necessarily involved the abandon-
ment of the illusion of transparency which, as Terry Hale argues, 'tends to
conceal a reductive process by which a text is made to assume local
cultural values'.[77] Free of the encumbrance of maintaining this illusion,
Coffey deployed his energies in a creative way. In purely technical terms
few translators have captured the rhythm and the movement of French
poems as well as Coffey has and I think he attached as much importance
to this aspect of translation as he did to rendering meanings. Indeed, as
these translations show, it almost seems as if this close attention to form,
rhythm and syntax enabled him to probe deeply into the meaning of the
poem and uncover its ambiguities while laying bare its inherent tensions.

Every translator brings his own values to bear on his or her translations
yet few are prepared to admit them openly. Coffey's values are plainly
those of the Christian Existentialist, therefore I believe he regarded the act
of translating not just as a technical challenge but as a philosophical and
moral one too. Honesty and fidelity rather than fluency and transparency
are the conditions of Coffey's model of translation: fidelity in the sense
that he cannot base his critique on something spurious; honesty in the
sense that he must be true to his own values and proclaim his presence
when he brings those values to bear on his translation.

# 4

# SOUND AND METRICS
# IN *ADVENT* (1975) AND
# *DEATH OF HEKTOR* (1982)

Brian Coffey's late poems deal with issues that are important to anyone concerned for the future welfare of humankind, but in order to experience their full meaning the reader must attend to the way they sound. Musical analogies come readily to mind while attempting to describe the essential qualities of Coffey's verse because he was, as I have argued, a musical poet. This may seem like an odd claim considering that one commentator wrote that his late poetry was 'minimalist', bare to the point of a 'seeming barrenness of effect' and lacking in 'euphonies and harmonies'.[1] Nevertheless, despite Coffey's reputation as a formidably cerebral poet, there is a sense in which one can speak of the physical experience of reading a poem like *Death of Hektor* (1982). Attentive readers of these long poems will experience a heightened consciousness of how the organs of vocal production must work to enunciate particular sounds. Another related effect of hearing the way Coffey makes words resonate is a renewed awareness of the materiality of language.

Anyone familiar with the full corpus of his work will know that a certain quality of sound has distinguished Coffey's poetry since he found his voice in *Third Person* (1938). Despite the many merits of this early collection new readers of Coffey would be better advised to begin with a work like *Death of Hektor*. Although it is a highly innovative poem, it deals with immediately recognisable themes and, unlike the much anthologised *Missouri Sequence* (1962), it exemplifies those special qualities that distinguish Coffey's best work. Coming as it does midway between an extraordinarily prolific decade that began with the long poem *Advent* (1975) and ended with the publication of his last collection *Chanterelles* (1985), *Death of Hektor* deals with some of the themes of *Advent* while developing many of the formal innovations discovered during the composition of that work. Conceived on a less grand scale than the earlier long poem, *Death of Hektor* is also concerned with such issues as human ecology, war, historiography and poetry, but it uses its Homeric subject matter to evolve a more compact argument. Both poems make creative use of vertical and horizontal space and their long lines resonate with allusions to other writers and strike echoes from earlier passages. Yet despite these thematic and formal continuities, each of the long poems possesses its own metrics.

The sound of these long poems bears a closer resemblance to *Third Person* than to *Missouri Sequence*. The verse is unpunctuated – this does bear on the rhythm and pace of Coffey's poetry – and dense sound patterning and syntactic experiment once again feature. While the tight, elliptical structures of *Third Person* were perfect vehicles for a poetry of compressed thought, the enlarged thematic scopes of *Advent* and *Death of Hektor* require a longer line, one capable of articulating fuller, more explicit utterances. While the extended reach of these lines permits arguments to unfold gradually and more discursively, it also enables narratives to be delivered in a way that allows Coffey to convey simultaneously his different responses to the action described.

Generally speaking, line breaks tend to coincide with grammatical or phrasal units which build into stanzas that constitute complete statements. In *Advent*, groups of stanzas form larger groupings or cantos which are separated from each other by a triple space. The principle that governs the order of cantos may be easily discerned as in parts 4 and 6. More often, each successive canto overlays the previous one with a different approach to a shared theme or with a series of illustrations, so that these cantos succeed and relate to each other like notes in a gradually extending chord. 'Subject-rhymes' or analogies lend an inner cohesion to each part and they are repeated across these parts so that the whole poem seems to be built out of a series of large-scale parallels or correspondences, with each correspondence defining itself in opposition to, or counter-balancing another.[2] Because there is literally more to hear in *Advent*, distinctive metres and phonetic sounds rarely travel beyond an individual part whereas long-range echoes and rhythmic leitmotifs such as the cretic (/ x /) are integral to the meaning of *Death of Hektor*.

The relationship between the stanzas that make up each of the fifteen short parts or page units that comprise *Death of Hektor* is governed by the way the poem maintains a dialogue between the past and the present. A single page may juxtapose different perspectives which shift across time and space. In page 11, for example, an extended space separates a description of the site upon which Troy once stood from a catalogue of images, the last of which focuses on the microscopic event of 'white cells battening upon the watering helpless blood'.[3] The importance of the page as a structural device cannot be overstated. By applying pressure on the

The emblematic bird featured on the front cover of the Brian Coffey special issue of the *Irish University Review*, published in Spring 1975. Birds frequently figure in Coffey's poetry and several people who had the privilege of knowing him personally remember him as 'birdlike'.

clearly demarcated narrative and discursive units it frames, each page points up a dialogic relationship which may not be immediately apparent. The most significant dialogue is articulated through sounds and rhythms which echo down the page and link these discrete units in a way that promotes the argument of the poem.

Lacking the organising effect that full end-rhyme has upon the line, *Advent* and *Death of Hektor* feature a variety of devices which magnetise the elements of their metrical structures. Intricate patterns of alliteration and assonance, and processes like sequence and chiasmus bind individual lines and link these lines into cohesive stanzas. The following passage from *Advent II* is typical in this respect.

> There they watch faithful earth maternal yield us our daily bread
> in such a place of passionate symbiosis
> man beast plant stone in all togetherness
> our nostrils quiver our breath caught 'God' we cry
>
> Not for us that natural use of taking yielding
> We rip the fruit untimely from the womb sing no filial praise
> Rapers peepers whippers cheaters thieves one and all
> stick the boot cold play like murder into stripped girl

> (PV 118)

Almost every sound participates in the overall effect here. In the first two lines the words 'they', 'faithful', 'daily' and 'place' are linked by assonance, while the second syllable of 'maternal' echoes the word that precedes it. The second line contains a good example of what Benjamin Hrushovski calls an 'expressive' sound pattern or 'sound metaphor', in which a particular sound combination represents a certain tone of content 'abstracted from the domain of meaning'.[4] Embedded in the insistent sibilance is the chiastic cluster SPPS which is mirrored in the syllables of 'symbiosis'. Another interesting feature is the way the repeated sounding of the cluster TRNS in 'TogetheRNeSS'/ 'NoSTRilS'/ 'NoT foR uS' and 'NaTuRal uSe' provides an important link between the two stanzas. This particular group modulates into a cognate cluster RPS which is developed through 'RiP', 'RaPeRS', 'PeePeRS', 'whiPPeRS' and 'StRiPPed'. Hrushovski argues that such 'focusing' sound patterns call attention to 'a relation between several sound clusters' and in this case the device points up man's radically altered relationship with the earth.

The way syntax and grammar combine to support sense is a function of the long line and the lack of punctuation. Without non-alphabetical marks to guide and direct phrasing, the reader is drawn more fully into the line and in the process of negotiating important ambiguities he discovers added dimensions of meaning. The symbiotic relationship between man and the earth is nicely conveyed by the ambiguity of 'faithful' which is simultaneously in apposition to 'they' and 'earth'. This line is typical of *Advent* in the way that successive words modify those that preceded them so that additional meanings are continually being generated by our retrospective reading. The adverbial function of 'faithful' is activated by the unexpected appearance of another adjective after the noun 'earth'; the verb 'yield' then exerts a pull on 'maternal' suggesting that it could equally function as an adverb. We might also note how, by subtle allusion to the Lord's Prayer, the invocation 'earth maternal yield us our daily bread' catches the eye so that 'earth' is felt to function simultaneously as the subject of one grammatical unit and the object of another. On the other hand, the unambiguous grammar of the sixth line, thematically the antithesis of the first, clearly establishes a new relationship, one in which the 'womb' of 'maternal earth' is now understood as a passive object.

Yet strict antithesis is not permitted here, at least not in the way we might initially suppose, and the way the sound of one stanza overlaps the other is reflected in the unusual use of pronouns. In one sense 'they' of stanza one are defined in opposition to 'we' of the next. This apparent opposition is complicated by the appearance of 'us' rather than the expected pronoun 'them' in line one. One might feasibly suggest that 'us' is used in the two stanzas to signify the human race considered dia-chronically, in which case man is understood as the enduring, yet no longer grateful, beneficiary of 'faithful earth's' bounty. The reader must remember, however, that what has been presented in the first stanza is one of many 'framed' scenes that *Advent* presents: the watchers are ourselves 'as it were dream[ing] back those golden realms' (*PV* 118). Intoxicated by idealised constructions of the past, we are apt to become disappointed with the real present and to forget 'old gods rivers peaks trees that see us born and die' (*PV* 117). Beauty is immanent in the 'unframed' natural world and we discover that Coffey is less concerned with the contrast between an Edenic past and a drab present than he is with two anti-thetical modes of being in the world.

Out of this central antithesis he develops an argument about poetry which implicates Mallarmé by alluding to his sonnet 'Le vierge, le vivace et le bel aujourd'hui . . .' and *Un Coup de dés*. The implications of this argument are far reaching and new connections are continually being made. The allusion is subtle: there are no footnotes and the sonnet is heard in the distinctive sounds of Coffey's verse.

Through ice broken and final floating leaves a tide a wake
console lustre unframed candour of hardy light
the swan oh how clear green of lake covers sunken head
flows along downy neck contrasts with smoother wing
down laid by water on down water beads tumble in air
time after time white to green light green to white change
no stasis passage out no return like dart in flight

It is here in the passing swan beauty beauty swan
jade on down a flow going past not nothingness

(PV 120)

This beautiful passage is important for several reasons and it exemplifies those qualities that point up continuities between *Advent* and
*Third Person*. For example, long monosyllables with their conspicuous
vowel sounds ('oh how clear green of lake') recall poems like 'Amaranth'
and 'Patience No Memory', but now the stream of sound is more
extended and the texture is richer than in the crisp, truncated units of
these early poems. The long line permits a subtle interplay between visual
rhyme and sound rhyme: the repeated sequence of the swan's movements
is mirrored in the chiastic structures of the sixth line. In the previous line,
the 'down' of the swan is on the water in two senses, it rests on it and is
reflected by it; yet the water is also on the 'down' and this enclosed
circuit of mirroring is again reflected in the sound of the line.

Complex patterns of internal rhyme give each line its coherence. They
act as a counterbalance to suspended rhythms which are determined less
by accent than quantity and to a syntax which permits individual phrases
and words to float freely. In the first line, certain sounds in the fragment
'ice broken' are echoed in 'final floating' and 'tide a wake'; 'console lustre'
finds an echo in 'candour', a word whose etymology provides a semantic
rhyme and conveys the radiance of the swan. Sibilants and hard 'k' sounds
in the third and fourth lines focus attention on the sense of 'contrasts'.

The variegation and transcience of the natural world are the key points
in this affirmation of natural beauty and its sounds, rhythms and
kinaesthetic imagery anticipate the early sections of *Death of Hektor*.
Significantly, the swan and the water on which it floats are not presented
as figure and ground. The colour and the movement of the water blend
fluidly with the swan to create an inscape. This is a consistent feature of
the other images of natural beauty that *Advent II* presents: a single violet
is situated in 'green shade'; a ladybird sits 'afloat on oak-leaf barque' and
a distant gull is 'wind-tossed at grey white-toothed wave'.

I discuss this passage at some length because the way it connects up
with other far-flung material is paradigmatic of *Advent* and different from

the way the units of *Death of Hektor* interact. In *Advent*, our ability to make necessary connections depends on our ability to recognise when a significant echo has been struck against sounds and images that hang in the memory. Beyond the phonetic sounds of the passage there is of course the allusion to Mallarmé's sonnet; however, subsequent material will prompt a retrospective understanding of the passage. From these tightly focused lines the verse expands into a generalised argument about time and mortality, and proceeds to expose the vacuous pride of the nihilist by way of pointed references to *Un Coup de dés,* a work which ultimately argues that negation is the only absolute.

> If as one peers in mirrors one's features age and age
> fear of no future absolute invites to court absurdity
> tempts to assert naught all naught now inverted hybris
> naught what has pleased ear and eye what pleases now
> only some abstract where of thinking for Beauty pure
>
> (PV 121)

The argument accumulates and the bulk of what *Advent II* has said thus far about man's alienation from the world and from his fellow man is brought to bear on an aesthetic that is now regarded from an unusual perspective. Lines 3–4 above echo the allusion to Aquinas's 'Tertia Via' which appeared towards the end of *Advent I*: 'think total voiding all whatever naughted and you too/ if once all with us were naught/ could aught ever be' (PV 116). Long-range phonetic echoing is rare in *Advent*, yet conspicuous self-echoing in the earlier passage accounts for its particular resonance and, while it made no pronouncements about poetic values, re-echoed in this new context it identifies the first principles of an aesthetic that is rooted in Catholic thought.[5] By means of visual rhyme, through which Coffey recalls the swan by depicting another bird several lines later – a 'gull wind-tossed at grey white-toothed wave' (PV 121) – the swan is now understood retrospectively as a symbol of created beauty and is set in opposition to the swan in Mallarmé's sonnet which functioned as a symbol of an abstract beauty, 'that other inferred'. The passage is perhaps the most explicit poetic expression of Coffey's aesthetic and it stresses the importance of the senses in the appreciation of the beauty of the sacramental world: 'beauty matched to us eye and ear colour sound and touch' (PV 121). Maritain's remark that the 'divination of the spiritual in the things of sense, and which expresses itself in the things of sense, is what we properly call POETRY' is a useful gloss on *Advent II*.[6]

Analogy and subject-rhyme operate in a similar way to visual and aural rhyme. In *Advent II*, the ambivalent Aisling, Petrarch's Laura and the ice-bound Symbolist swan, can now be seen or heard as harmonising parts of a series which is balanced by another series that includes the floating swan, the 'bent-zen-print-twig' wife, and the shepherd's harp which gives 'voice to star and sky'. The analogies that make up the first series are posited as different expressions of misguided human ambition. New and unsettling links are continually exposed and the reader is invited to ponder the possible relationship between Mallarmé's quest for an absolute beauty and man's alienation from the earth. Retrospective discovery of significant links by way of an expanded understanding of rhyme is an important constitutive principle of *Advent*. It is for this reason that the poem demands to be read in a single reading because each part of *Advent* is significantly modified by others. The shorter parts that make up *Death of Hektor* are also interdependent but their relationship is governed by a different principle, one that admits of a dialogue between the past and the present all the while moving forward through time.

In *Death of Hektor*, each part seems to follow on naturally from the previous one, much like the stages of a single coherent argument; in *Advent*, parts often end interrogatively, obliquely anticipating the opening of the next part. *Advent I* concludes with a question from which the reader infers a situation like that dramatised in *Waiting for Godot*. The opening of *Advent II* responds with a question about an imagined arrival; however, this time the long awaited visitants are ourselves, conscious that our presence has been greeted, but unable to comprehend the significance of this greeting. The question that closes this second part ('who shall inscribe in sand man's secret heart') is followed by an argument about history that is based on Aristotle's dictum that 'poetry is something more philosophical and more worthy of serious attention than history; for while poetry is concerned with universal truths, history treats of particular facts.'[7] *Advent III* concludes with another question 'who could tell the story to its end', to which *Advent IV* responds by speculating on the implications of a future visitation by 'unkin others'.

An important feature of the sound of these early parts is the way allusions are forcibly detached from their original contexts and often cited to reinforce an argument that their respective authors might have never endorsed. The allusion to Eliot's *Gerontion* – 'History has many cunning passages, contrived corridors/ And issues, deceives with whispering ambitions, . . .' – in the opening stanzas of *Advent III* is plainly corroborative. In the next part, telling allusions to 'Easter 1916' reinterpret Yeats's sense of historical change and imply a link between his response to the events of 1916 and our likely response to the arrival of hypothetical visitants, the 'unkin others'.

> If they should come   unkin others
>
> perhaps in lightning
> out of clear sky
> and gentler then their landfall
> than wind-born feather-fall to water
>
> For us awakened
> all changed changed utterly
>
> *(PV 129)*

This allusion is later echoed to establish a parallel between these two responses –Yeats's and ours – and the response of the 'unkin others' to a 'voice [that] broke sleep in them' *(PV 131)*. These links prompt an evaluation of the degree to which each response is based on an accurate understanding of what has in fact taken place and the reader must draw the correct moral from each one. In the final instance a message, whose meaning foreshadows that of the central figure of Christ in *Advent VIII*, has wakened these 'unkin others' but the subsequent narrative establishes a rhyme with all those other instances in *Advent* where people wake 'from sleep to sleep' *(PV 111)*. Misunderstanding the voice, the 'unkin others' are allured by 'the spell of some great deed' which precipitates the despoliation of their planet. So, while the relevance of *Advent IV* may seem tenuous at first reading, it contains some of the most significant writing in *Advent* and the moral of these rhymed narratives is amplified by the sequence of aphorisms and rhetorical questions with which the part concludes:

> Mute is the lute in absent wind if lutanist
> has tired of lute in laodicean sleep
>
> Sterile the seed that drops in sand dry as mummy queen
>
> . . . . . . . . . . . .
>
> Do we live a sleep we must be raised from
> or else sleep on
>
> *(PV 132)*

One does not have to hear the scriptural echoes in these stanzas to know that at this point the poem has turned to the central theme of what it is that true awakening involves – namely, receptivity and a readiness to engage totally. The arrival of the 'unkin others' and their history are ironic devices, designed to objectify the way our reponse to events is determined by the degree to which we feel they advance or threaten our misguided ambitions. Spiritual awakening will not occur if we mistake our wants for our needs and as long as we proceed on the assumption that human beings must define themselves through the struggle to realise ambitions that are ultimately unrealisable we effectively remain asleep. The end of *Advent IV* releases a moral that resonates across the remainder of the poem and bears decisively on some of the final stanzas of the final part. The example of the 'unkin others', who had left their 'planet gutted', casts an ominous shadow over *Advent V* which deals with humankind's potentially ruinous failure to appreciate earth's beauty and bounty.

So far, *Advent* has examined the value of humanity's collective response to the challenges of living in this world. From this point on, the poem focuses on personal reminiscence. *Advent VI* celebrates the quality of a mother's response to the trials of life and the grace with which she accepted the inevitability of her death. Coffey then moves on to meditate on the death of his son and to examine why this son adopted a mode of living which precipitated his death.[8]

The type and quality of analyses that distinguish the first six parts of *Advent* are a function of its moral and political perspective and it is a testament to Coffey's courage that he should even attempt to apply the values that the poem has upheld thus far in this analysis of a deeply painful experience. Occuring as it does within the natural cycle of events, the death of a mother is felt to be inevitable: it does not challenge faith like the untimeliness of the death of a son. The mother in *Advent VI* is an exemplary figure and her life and death reaffirm the Christian-Existentialist argument of the poem. This argument finally strains in *Advent VII*, however, because the evaluative thrust that the poem has generated cannot be brought to bear fully on subject matter that is hardly – and many would say, ought not to be – susceptible to this kind of treatment. To put it another way, if the values that have informed the life and the displaced poetic vision of a father are felt to be implicated in the misguided choices of a son, then this requires the type of rigorous self-analysis that could call into question the validity of that vision and the values that inform it.

*Advent VII* raises more questions than it can answer and the complexities and obscurities that characterise much of its syntax are symptomatic of a struggle to maintain an impossible critical distance on a subject of such immediate relevance. Tonalities are often difficult to discern and there is an uneasy sense that feelings of guilt and anger have been repressed so that the part can be made to align with a larger structure that is pre-destined to culminate in a gesture of acceptance. Many of these feelings, particularly those directed against an outdated heroic ideology, are more satisfactorily articulated in *Death of Hektor*. Less personally involving, the subject matter of that poem can be held at a fixed distance so that tonalities can be brought to a sharper focus, and syntax and form can respond more fluidly to poetic feeling.

As I have argued, some of the passages in *Advent VII* are clouded in obscurity and at times it is difficult to discern whether the part is intended as act of self-examination or if the life and death of a son are the principal subjects of enquiry. Its opening lines illustrate the point and it is not easy to establish what they deny or affirm.

> Not every book not flesh full sad and proud
> of hopelessness not bumsteer wild escape
> through garden gate to sailors singing charms
>
> not at all to shut invincible eyes
> hand self lies open self-abyss on naught's night
>
> (*PV* 140)

The unmistakeable, but nonetheless confusing, allusion to Mallarmé's 'Brise Marine' is possibly employed to discriminate between the Symbolist's preference for an unworldly imaginative realm and the renunciation of one for whom death was an attractive alternative to the compromising ways of life. Yet readers could be forgiven for thinking that the denial woven into this reference to 'Brise Marine', whose speaker, a poet, is momentarily tempted into a dereliction of familial responsibility, seems more pertinent to the father than to his son.[9]

A series of visual patterns provides a parallel commentary on the part as it unfolds. A butterfly emerges from a chrysalis and later expands to signify a wider consciousness of nature and culture. The sequence finally contracts into a coffin shape made up of words with largely morbid connotations. While some the the words that constitute each of these patterns are selected from various parts of *Advent*, the patterns themselves do not interact creatively with the surrounding text, nor do their respective words relate with each other in a way that signifies anything beyond what we already know from the stanzas that they accompany. Because *Advent VII* fails to confront many of the questions it raises, the reader approaches the final part with a heightened sense of expectation. While the different metrics of the opening pages of *Advent VIII* do argue for a sense of arrival, one is left with the feeling that the poem has skirted, rather than bridged, a yawning gap.

Wake at last to like an old planet
dry far from its sun
dust driven no grass
in faint light shadow fainter
and sight arrested halt

Squat hill daubed red
black streaked and chill
sky backdrop unfeatured
north south east west
zenith black

The very place itself still
what more real
for each one alone what now to ask

(PV 145)

The first thing that the reader will notice is the look of the lines on the page. Lines and stanzas are shorter, and this conveys an impression of decisive movement. Our ear quickly confirms this visual impression of difference. The elaborate assonantal patterning of the longer line is dispensed with in favour of closed monosyllablic words, many of which feature consonants belonging to the 'hard' end of the scale. Other features such as the slow phrasal rhythm, the strict conjunction of lines and elliptical syntactic units, the use of frequent pauses within these shorter lines and the austere imagery all combine to create a verse form that stands in stark relief against the background of the preceding parts

Lacking a subject, the first stanza prompts the question 'Who is this person that wakes to like an old planet?' By recalling the opening line of *Advent*, Coffey establishes an important point of reference from which we can evaluate the difference between two types of wakefulness, both of which are really antithetical modes of being. The 'unfeatured unrapturing deep' of the first stanza of *Advent I* is recalled in the 'unfeatured' sky that now serves as a backdrop to a scene whose composition will determine the structure and the thematic focus of much of *Advent VIII*. To hear the way this final part simultaneously echoes, yet clearly differs, from *Advent 1* is to understand what Coffey hoped to achieve overall. While *Advent I* ranges across massive expanses of imagined time and space, and examines in chronological order a series of images that record humankind's 'upward path', it finally culminates in a reductive analysis of where this path has led to. The panoramic sweep of this movement can uncover no positive vision and the apparent freedom with which the verse moves through time is continually undermined by images of confinement, alienation and suppressed utterance.

> From tumbled citadel one stared at air
> shaped by walls        rigid like speech frozen
>
> (*PV* 111)

> Women alone men alone        barefaced the walls
> constraint and blind eyes to play the guide
>
> (*PV* 113)

While searching questions express a wish and suggest a possible solution, they also imply a present state of constraint and spiritual depletion:

> How to turn off helplessness and waking face
> like eagle soaring the hopelessness that sours clay
>
> (*PV* 114)

Unlike *Advent I*, the opening pages of *VIII* do not feature scenes that dissolve and recede; instead, form is determined by an image that signifies something beyond the ken of human experience, an image capable of sustaining prolonged meditation. Three icons are described as the eye moves with a new sense of direction from left to right and finally to the central figure of the crucified Christ; the sound of the lines give this vision a hard-edged clarity that all the others lacked. Having described this central figure the poem dwells upon its meaning, and the ease with which the lines now move contrasts dramatically with the stanzas of *Advent I* where syntactic, verbal and rhythmic ambiguity expressed doubt and indirection. The range of movements permitted by this form given from without are freely chosen and the paradox is that to 'Stay at centre' is to enjoy a freedom and a clarity of vision not accessible to those who follow 'line of want's aim' (*PV* 148).

Read in isolation, lines like 'We are always in human circumstances/ no angels and prone to forget/ we can work only from point to point' (*PV* 149) might seem to rehearse self-evident truths and as such barely seem worth quoting. Yet the displaced perspective from which Coffey regards and evaluates history, culture and politics throughout *Advent I* to *V* and the way these parts interact to establish the coherence of this perspective gives these lines an authority they would otherwise lack. Reading them, we might remember the Symbolist poet's desire to create a pure 'Beauty' which is ultimately 'in gift of none', the arrogance of those historians who 'surface to shout if p then q' and the 'unkin others' of *Advent IV* who, like us, sought to establish mastery over 'what now they saw fulfilled without them'.

This is the type of effect that *Advent* continually endeavours to create. Its structural units, both large and small, are mutually interdependent, each part modifying, and being modified by the others and its form is determined by the nature of its vision. It is a poem of insight rather than blinding revelation and this is utterly consistent with Coffey's existentialist understanding of Christian faith. The poem is specially designed to facilitate a system of correspondences that release insights by bringing into new and unusual relations the available facts of the human condition. What enables these relations to be perceived is that the facts that constitute them are all regarded from a singularly moral standpoint. As the poem advances and as more relations come into view this perspective is continually affirmed. The one significant weak point in the poem occurs when an event calls into question the very values upon which this point of view is based.

*Advent* finally describes how it is, yet it does not say why it should be so, for if it were to attempt to do this it would contradict the very principles by which it makes its discoveries. The poem finally identifies a lack which it cannot fill by inferring beyond the known facts: 'No quick foxy soothers wanted here/real words fail darling thought/ though all is plain' (*PV* 149). Constrained by its own logic, *Advent* cannot make the type of claims that Mallarmé made for poetry by effecting some kind of all-transcending synthesis and it is this necessary flaw that accounts for the feeling of anti-climax that we experience reading its final stanzas.

*     *     *

While it picks up and develops further many of the techniques discovered during the writing of *Advent*, the more restricted scope and steady focus of *Death of Hektor* make it less susceptible to the kind of criticisms offered above. The later poem examines issues raised in *Advent* such as the Aristotelian argument concerning history and poetry, the dangers of an outdated heroic code and the recurring theme of man's despoliation of earth. *Death of Hektor* employs a long line that contracts and expands around a norm of five stresses – unlike *Advent* where the norm was six – and lines are organised into unrhymed groupings that generally comprise three to six lines. Once again, sound patterning lends these lines cohesion and although their syntax is characteristically elliptic their meanings are accessible. I set these down as norms, but, in *Death of Hektor*, structure and form are more immediately responsive to states of feeling than in *Advent*, and intensities of emotion can often be measured by the degree to which the verse departs from these norms.

Strict pagination of the numbered parts allows Coffey to develop an interplay between text and vertical space and the establishment of the page as a unit of meaning creates a new and more dynamic interaction between the separate groupings that occupy it. The rhythms of rising and falling that are continually sounded through the poem are matched by the way the first line of each successive page unit begins higher or lower on the page so that the poem visually describes a series of peaks and troughs.[10]

The opening of the poem, with its clear echoes from *Hamlet*, raises questions about truth, perspective and relevance:

> Of what we are to Hektor     Nothing to say
>
> Of Hektor to us
>
> (*DH* 1)

Why, we might ask, does Coffey not open simply with the single question '[Of] what is Hektor to us [?]'. This is, after all, the essential question that the poem addresses. By adopting the strategy of posing a question, answering it unequivocally in the negative, then inverting the subject and object of that question to form another which remains unanswered, Coffey creates a space which elicits from the reader a number of possible answers, each one silently articulated with an interrogative inflection: 'Nothing [to say]?', 'Something?' or 'Everything?'. The answer as question, or rather the answer that proceeds by acknowledging the difficulty of the question that prompted it, is thus posited as a different kind of response. This is not to say that the poem proceeds by 'aporia pure and simple'.[11] By clearing a space for such a response this opening authorises an imaginative excursion into the past.

The type of truth that *Death of Hektor* will define is available only to a poet like Homer, who achieves a 'depth of insight into the human condition' while 'remaining immersed in the detail of place and time'.[12] For Coffey, Homer's portrayal of Achilles and Mayakovsky's character-isation of Lenin had succeeded where the *Táin* and Yeats had failed because both poets had 'contrive[d] to express the unawakened spirit of people imprisoned in narrowness'. This relates back to the complex mechanism that prompts the poem. The essential truth of what Homer has to say about the human condition and the source of its relevance for us today cannot be uncovered by the principles of scholarship because these principles are not directed towards the real locus of meaning. The opening lines create a dramatic silence in which we search and probe for a fitting response so that the reader is made aware of the value and meaning of certain types of silence. *Death of Hektor* attends to the silences in which significant meanings resonate in Books XXI and XXII of the *Iliad*.[13] Listening to these silences and drawing the inferences that they invite, Coffey arrives at a very personal – some would say eccentric – understanding of Homer's epic, one in which Hektor, rather than Achilles, emerges as the morally heightened stoic hero.[14]

Coffey's approach to the epic is continuous with his method of translation and with the principles that informed the composition of *Advent*. He uses poetry and translation to test and inscribe values, and he adopts a displaced yet nonetheless enabling perspective, one through which new and unsettling links can be identified. The essential differences between the two poems can be best explained in terms of their respective metrics. The distinctions that Pound draws between two types of poetic counterpoint best illustrate the different ways that these long poems create their particular sounds. Pound discusses the contrapuntal texture of Provençal metrical schemes which culminate in

> a sort of horizontal instead of perpendicular chord. One might call it a 'sort of' counterpoint; if one can conceive a counterpoint which plays not against a sound newly struck, but against the residuum and residua of sounds which hang in the auditory memory.[15]

Adapting Pound's terminology one might say that the cantos and parts of *Advent* make up a series of horizontal chords. Analogies and sounds linger as 'residua' in the memory against which echoes can be struck over a long distance. The fifteen pages that comprise *Death of Hektor* can be usefully compared to 'perpendicular chords' made up of lines and units that exist in a significant relationship with others placed beneath or above them. The following two stanzas from page 1 can be usefully analysed in terms of the way their sounds and structures are vertically related.

> From unwitnessed unwitnessable start
> *void* naming a 'nothing exists'
> *time* the noun no substantive
> how slowly-swiftly time does move
> now as walls crumbling through centuries
> now as lightning out of the east
>
> A vantage point in unrecorded past
> supposes Hektor seen from ages off
>                    (*DH* 1, Coffey's italics)

In the first stanza a counterpoint is established between the sentence which moves linearly and the vertically stacked metrical units over which it is draped. The visual line plays an important role in punctuating the stanza into six discrete units. Constructed grammatically, the stanza opens with a prepositional phrase, followed by two lines which function like parenthesised descriptions of 'start'; line 4 delivers a main clause while the next two are adverbial clauses modifying 'move'. The first line creates an expectation which is not fulfilled until line four and this suspension of the main clause heightens our sense of a long-awaited progression from stasis to movement. This progression is mirrored by the way that time, finally emerging out of the 'void' as it were, releases a series of kinaesthetic images. Significant echoes are sounded in equivalent line positions: consonance links the end-words 'substantive', 'move' and 'off', while 'east' is echoed in the near rhyme 'past'; assonance of 'i' sounds links 'exists' and 'substantive' as it does the long 'e' sounds in 'centuries' and 'east'; alliteration of the consonantal cluster 'st' connects 'start', 'exists', 'substantive', 'east' and 'past'; finally, the long vowel sound 'ow' is repeated through three consecutive lines (4–6) in similar positions.

Few other passages in the poem are characterised by such dense echoing of sounds in similar line positions, yet different species of rhyme at line-ends recur with much greater regularity than in *Advent* and it becomes an important principle in the sound structure of the poem. This is not to suggest that end rhyme displaces sound-patterns heard across the line; rather, the devices are mutually reinforcing and both will later participate fully in the aural drama of the central movements, working with rhythm and syntax to give the lines a clamour and a dynamic that distinguish them from anything heard in *Advent*. The important thing to note about the stanza in question is that the interplay of its lines anticipates the way subsequent passages will create their larger effects: obvious syntactic parallelism and anaphora in lines 5–6 prefigure the long central stanza in page 10; stressed italicised nouns at the beginning of lines 2 and 3 resonate across the rest of the line much as 'Doom' and 'Fate' will echo out over whole stanzas later on.

The usefulness of the analogy with musical counterpoint is that it can accommodate inner differences and new dynamic elements within a consistent texture. In musical counterpoint, melodies may follow the same contours but they could also diverge to opposite ends of the tonal register; consonance can modulate into dissonance, while rhythms may move in unison or play against each other. In each instance the texture of the piece remains the same. The analogy between music and poetry is, of course, essentially fallacious. In poetry we can only hear one line being sounded at a time so one has to be careful not to force comparisons where they might not apply. But poetry can aspire to the condition of counterpoint when poets make vowels, consonants and rhythms resonate far beyond their immediate sounding so that sounds 'newly struck' can be heard simultaneously with others stored in the mind's ear. One of the curious features of *Death of Hektor* is that its lines and stanzas demand to be heard in conjunction with previous lines and stanzas. Coffey's deepest poetic intuition is to bind all his clearly demarcated sounds, his strange rhythms and dislocated syntax into intricate patterns so that nothing is abandoned. Furthermore, he creates an environment in which echoes can be heard in dissimilar contexts. The unproblematic syntax and perfect iambic pentameters that close page I contrast with the crossed rhythms and ambiguities of the other stanzas to express a sense of achieved perspective but while they do stand apart from the other stanzas, these iambic lines continue a sequence of subtly modulating end rhymes.

Page 2 better exemplifies what I am describing. Composed of three stanzas it juxtaposes two contrasting styles of writing. Mimetic in its primal rhythms and sounds, the first defines itself as an essentially *poetic* mode. There is oxymoron ('unhushed quiet'); some of the lines have an incantatory quality and the verse is marked by an Aristotelian preference for compressed metaphor. The rhythms of the second style are almost prose-like by comparison and its more conventional grammatical structures and extended simile identify the mode as *discursive*. One mode intuits the past and implicitly makes claims for poetry while the other acknowledges the epistemological conditions that circumscribe man's attempt to construct the past. The poem gains in truth by recognising the difficulty of its undertaking.

A large vertical space establishes the distance that separates past and present yet sounds and rhythms from the past echo *down* this silence and resonate in the present. Echo thus becomes a metaphor for poetry itself and the two modes that comprise this part interact and reinforce an implicit argument. Here is the first stanza of page 2:

> Rise and fall      earth and water
> to and fro      waves of sea
> climate not weather to shelter land from fire
> sun-glow shapes cloud-cover      fills air
> all is benignity      swan-down for cygnets
> yet in the unhushed quiet it moves
> it moves      it flows
> wear away wear away      earth air water fire
> time like Camber sand blown a prairie fire below the dunes

One could argue that this stanza reflects Coffey's interest in early Greek philosophy yet much of its meaning resides in the type of physical responses it elicits from the reader. In the first two lines space halts the process of signification or, better, it calls attention to another and equally important mode of signification. By foregrounding the sound of each phrase, silence invites the reader to reflect on the way that the organs of vocal production must work to enunciate their respective sounds. In addition to spacing, the high proportion of stressed monosyllables slows down delivery so that each word is heard separately and attended to literally one at a time. Note for example how the simple verbs 'rise' and 'fall' take on a new mimetic force if we mark the physical sensation of rising and falling felt in the mouth as we produce their respective vowel sounds. Newly sensitised to the act of vocal production, the reader is now aware of the tongue rising from 'fall' to articulate the high vowel sound in 'earth' and retracting towards the soft palate to repeat the back vowel 'a' in 'water'. In the following line attention switches to the lips as they move forward and backward – literally 'to and fro'– to produce a carefully chosen sequence of vowels. Perhaps the most noteworthy example of what I am describing here occurs in the last line of the stanza: 'a prairie fire below the dunes'. Here the place of articulation moves systematically from high ('prairie') to low ('dunes') to convey the sense of 'below'. Language thus becomes the medium through which the reader mimics earth's geophysical rhythms, and these rhythms continue to reverberate throughout these opening pages.[16] The cretic foot is established as an important rhythmic leitmotif: it recurs in the eigth line ('Wear away wear away'); although only heard as a faint echo it closes page 2 ('long foreseen') and resounds through the stanzas of pages 4 and 5.

As we would expect, sounds recur down through the stanza. Each of the salient vowel pairings in line two are heard several lines later yet each echo is differently struck: line 7 draws out the first phrase ('to and fro') by interposing a silence between the modulated 'o' sounds ('it moves      it flows'); the salient vowels in 'waves of sea' are contracted into the single word 'prairie' in line 9. Despite the densely echoic quality of the stanza, there is a continual interplay between its sharply contrasting timbres. Note, for example, how the soft and hard consonants of 'sun-glow shapes cloud cover' play against each other to point up the contrast between the transparency of light and the opacity of the cloud. Again, sound promotes an unstated yet important theme of the poem: through a creative interaction of different elements and reciprocal movements nature has shaped an environment capable of sustaining life – 'all is benignity'.

Contrasts in quantity also contribute to the sound of the stanza. Open syllables ending with long vowels, and monosyllables that contain long vowels and diphthongs dominate the rhythms of the opening two lines. Line three introduces disyllabic words and their shorter vowels are clearly separated by consonantal boundaries. Sound and quantity then combine to create a wonderful climax in line 8. Shorter syllables closed by dental consonants are briefly foregrounded and then placed in juxtaposition with longer closed syllables to create a sense of confined energy. This effect is intensified by the anticipation created by the line break and an unexpected repetition at the beginning of line 7. 'It flows' opens up the sound but maintains the dark tonal quality of those low vowels. The repeated, emphatic cretics and ringing vowels ('wear away      wear away') that follow on after such careful preparation are felt as a release of

2

Rise and fall     earth and water
to and fro     waves of sea
climate not weather to shelter land from fire
sun-glow shapes cloud-cover     fills air
all is benignity     swan-down for cygnets
yet in the unhushed quiet it moves
it moves     it flows
wear away wear away     earth air water fire
time like Camber sand blown a prairie fire below the dunes


We can not hold time fast in our sights
as if judging events in a moment unique
like hill-top watcher taking Battle in at a glance


We were not present to discover
how what it was became what it is
nor see how one performs freely the long foreseen

Pages 2–3 of *Death of Hektor*. The use of space, the employment of the page as a unit of meaning and the way the opening line of each successive unit begins higher or lower on the page to form an undulating pattern are integral to the poem.

3

For us it is point to point with pick and spade
scope and probe parchment perhaps to try
when luck holds      seldom clear-sky clear-say
blindways night rubble earthquake residues
the all too often often the all too much

It may be whom a moment's spotlight deifies
to tease appearances shows black white
white black dissolves bird in wind sky in dragons
himher into what is of tribal tale the maze

May be      Maybe      Dream it
We do not steer the stars

primordial energy and echoes of this climactic moment resonate in each of the named elements that complete the line. Phonetic, phrasal and rhythmic repetition combine with catalogue to give the line the quality of a chant and we can measure the distance the poem has already covered by returning to the first stanza of page I which, with its gently modulating sounds ('scant' – 'wind' – 'friend') and tentative rhythms articulated by a voice that speaks out of personal experience, is as close as Coffey gets to sounding like a conventional lyric poet.

The backward movement through time, then, is as much about affirming the truth of poetry by reconnecting it with its vital origins as it is an attempt to establish a 'vantage point in unrecorded past'. It is in this context that we can understand the abrupt switch from the carefully sculpted pair of iambic pentameters that close page 1 – the iambic being, of course, the chief type of metre in most classical and modern prosody– into the primal rhythms of the next page.[17] A 'vantage point' is attained less through discursive thought than through poetic intuition.

The space that separates the first two stanzas signifies the expanse of time that separates the unrecorded past from the present, yet the two stanzas are linked by echoes. It is worthwhile juxtaposing the two lines that stand either side of this interlinear blank:

time like Camber sand blown a prairie fire below the dunes


We can not hold time fast in our sights

(DH 2)

The repetition of 'time' is an obvious link but there are other important echoes: reverse rhyme connects the first syllable of 'Camber' and 'can'; there is a chiasmus in 'blown' and 'hold'; 'We' echoes the second syllable in 'prairie'; 'fire'/'fast' and 'fire'/'sights' are linked by alliteration and assonance respectively. It is not simply the mere repetition of sounds that enable us to hear so many echoes; the slight junctures that separate the monosyllables in the second line allow just enough silence for each sound to be registered as an echo.

In his book *Reading Voices*, Garrett Stewart examines how a phonemic reading of texts effectively deconstructs the figure/ground model that we normally apply to the relationship between a signifying text and the supposedly inactive blank upon which it is inscribed. Stewart suggests that new literary effects will be produced if a reader incorporates the blank spaces that intervene between words and stanzas:

A word . . . may seem all over, all said, its figuring function lapsing back to
ground – when all of a sudden the next word just may, in waiting to emerge
at  the other side of the gaping ground, turn out to have been bound up
partially,  recursively, with the word we have just read, whose signifying
function it now  refigures at an unsettling off-angle to the tread of script.[18]

This is the type of reading that *Death of Hektor* seems to invite and the
passage describes exactly what happens between the two words separated
by the 'gaping ground' in page 3.

> It may be whom a moment's spotlight deifies
> to tease appearances shows black white
> white black dissolves bird in wind sky in dragons
> himher into what is of tribal tale the maze

> May be     Maybe     Dream it
> We do not steer the stars

(*DH* 3)

Here space points up a possible homophonic link between 'maze' and
'may(s)'. The reader is immediately drawn back to the preceding stanza
and when read retrospectively, this crucial last word acquires new layers
of meaning. The process of constructing and understanding the past is a
dynamic one and a transvaluation of values is apt to occur in which
black is likely to mutate into white and vice versa, so that every 'tribal
tale' could be considered as a 'maze' in which the facts about the past are
lost. Given this, the sum of propositions about the past implicit in any
rehearsal of the 'tribal tale' might equally be considered as a series of
'mays'. This technique can be considered as a highly compressed form of
the use of echo in *Advent*, where echoes struck against the residua of earlier
sounds prompt a retrospective understanding of intervening material.

   In page 13 echo through interlinear space emerges as the dominant
metaphor of the poem. Note how an initial sound is subtly amplified and
sustained through subsequent repetition so that its resonance can pierce
through several lines of text and down through a considerable period of
silence so that when it is struck again the reader has the impression of
hearing a distant echo:

Degree he knew reverence for degree     Not enough there
to slake mad anger so prayed prayer unavailing with Greeks
for decent burial at the hands of his kin
obtained later when grudging foe saw spoil and profit

Hektor across three thousand years your gasped plea
for befittingness has filled my ears since boyhood

(DH 13)

Shrill, open 'e''s are foregrounded in the first line and subsequent
repetition in 'Greeks' and 'decent' carry this sound through a din of other
vowel sounds ('prayed prayer unavailing'), plosives, velar consonants,
and on down through the space so that it resonates in the opening line of
the next stanza. What we are hearing in this second stanza is, of course,
Hektor's plea resonating three millennia later.

I wrote earlier that form in *Death of Hektor* was more responsive to
feeling than was the case in *Advent* and that the cohesion of the poem
had much to do with the way it traces a clearly discernible curve of
feeling. We are left with the impression of a work where emotions are
initially reigned in so that the conditions that circumscribe any attempt to
speak truthfully about the past can be fully acknowledged. Without
having to resort to outright assertion, this carefully orchestrated man-
oeuvre establishes the authority of poetry by redefining the way words
can impart truths: the portrait of that superior artist, Homer, will later
make explicit much that is implicit in these early parts.

The poem identifies and repeatedly validates the grounds of its truth.
Recurring use of the past tense in the opening stanzas of page 4
establishes the remoteness of the past yet the elemental metrics of page 2
are now assimilated into the verse. Note how the tongue works to
articulate 'The Day One of peak tip peeping' or how the high-low vowel
pairing in 'ionian ' is reversed in 'olympian ' in the fifth stanza to convey
the sense of 'trenches' and 'heights'. The cretic foot is continually
sounded: 'Time ere poems', 'up-and-down land and sea' and 'notice change
between the nodal crests'. What I say here holds good for page 5, which
resembles the preceding part in the way that it measures out its argument
in equivalent stanzas.

Readers who have so far incorporated the blank spaces into their
reading will sense a change of dynamic in page 6. From a stanza length

that rarely exceeded 6 lines we now move into a sustained utterance of 15 lines. The repetition of interrogative phrases and the insistent rising rhythm that cuts across the opening lines establishes a new momentum: ('Homer     where born where buried of whom the son/ what journeys undertaken not known'). This new tempo lapses but it is soon re-established: key words are repeated ('His ears open to spoken word and words down time like wind-blown sand/ words of triumph . . .'); syntactic parallelism and lists also feature ('Black night for death     Colours of morning evening for life/ the rose the glaucous the amethystine wave-work carpeting'). The earlier lines are punctuated by short pauses and capitals but as we progress through the stanza they appear with less fre-quency so that the second half of the stanza expands into a continuous soundstream that distinguishes the verse from *Advent*. So much momentum is generated across these long lines that consecutive monosyllables ('black white red of man at war') are swept along in a 'swirl of sound'.

Despite the graphic images of war, the poetry is suffused with the celebration of its subject, Homer, of whom history can tell us little. An allusion to Joyce opens up a new critical perspective on that writer and the source of the reference suggests that what Coffey is offering here is a portrait of another, superior artist. Homer did not regard his art from the detached position of an indifferent god, 'invisible, refined out of existence', nor did he adopt a mask like Yeats; his poetry stands as a testament to an apparently unmediated reception of the world:[19]

> He pared no fingernails not indifferent     not masked
> Light we suppose once had entered eyes to brand memory
> with noon's exact flame of sun mirrored in wind-stirred sea
>
> (*DH* 6)

Important echoes from page 2 are sounded here: Homer's inner eye records the interaction of the elements while the cretic foot dominates the rhythm of the third line. A wonderful circuit of mirroring – a recurring motif in *Third Person*, in which mirroring also has associations with the creative process – is established through sound and imagery. The poet's eyes reflect the 'flame of sun' which is reflected in the sea – an image that echoes the process of cloud formation described in page 2 – and this process of mirroring is given its aural analogue in the chiastic pattern, 'mi*rr*ored *in* wind-sti*rr*ed sea'. Sound mirrors the visual and the visual mirrors sound in a manner reminiscent of the swan passage in *Advent II*. Just as Homer's eyes had been open to light so were his ears open to the 'spoken word and words down time *like* wind-blown sand' [my italics]. Again, the elements are present in the imagery and the simile resonates with echoes of another simile from page 2: 'time like Camber sand blown'.

*Death of Hektor* features several extended passages, yet while there are similarities between each of these superbly orchestrated crescendos they all describe a different tonality. Beyond a certain point a sustained pitch of feeling can begin to lose its impact, and its effectiveness within the larger structure of the poem is a function of correct placement and contrast. Despite its diversity and inner variety, certain passages of *Advent* seem superfluous and they lack the dynamic that Coffey generates within the smaller structural frames or page units of *Death of Hektor*. The sustained but not overlong note of celebration sounded in the first stanza of page 6 is followed by one that interrogates the politics of literary reception. This question creates the context for the first stanza of page 7.

So far, the poem has proceeded through an interplay of discursive and chronologically sequenced descriptive passages. Page 7 is different for several reasons: its two constituent units are not obviously related – one does not comment explicitly on the other; secondly, it introduces a new narrative element into the poem. It accords with the established paradigm by bringing the past and the present into a single frame, but it inverts the chronology as it does the visual layout of the preceding page. The opening line highlights the complicity between the institutions of literary instruction and political authority: 'Tradition     Scholars     Establishment        Well-filled heads'. Yet what is the relationship between this critique of a discourse, which while it purports to be ideologically uncommitted in its quest for universal truths promotes the interests of particular groups, and the ensuing narrative?

Traditional critics would have us accept Achilles as the embodiment of the heroic code, and *Death of Hektor* is designed to unsettle our assumptions by balancing them against the facts as they are recorded in the *Iliad*. Coffey's narration of Achilles' slaughter of the Trojans does not go beyond what we already know from Book XXI but the manner of the telling is calculated to invoke values that are felt to be essential for the continuance of civilisation. These are values which are curiously elided in a scholarly discourse yet, as Chapman and Coffey would argue, they are implicit in the *Iliad*.

Priam watching from Troy Wall fearful felt the glare
light like Sirius white on the slaughter plain
nimbus      Achilles spher'd round with battle glory
luminous like Cuchullain figure of War Itself
belly-ripper head-splitter neck-lopper
skewering fighters commoners heroes alike
with ash-tree spear gift of his father weapon unique
what none but he could lift shake and throw
tossing from it corpses to river Xanthus choking it
cursing the dying mocking the dead      action man galore
of slaughter      mindless glory      embodied hatred's stench of blood
cool malice      merciless      Achaean paramount
true professional      he stares out his own death imminent
golden hair image of manhood for vain victorian dead souls
Achilles fleet of foot unloving he worships gory spoils
his unawakened spirit impassive under doom

*(DH 7)*

 This stanza achieves its particular effects in several ways. We see the unfolding spectacle from the same perspective as Priam. His fear is palpable in the rhythms and pauses of the opening two lines and because we are granted some access into his inner state he strikes us as being more fully human than the subject of his fear, Achilles. The single word 'nimbus' designates the aura of invincibility which surrounds the Achaean and it marks him out as the favourite of the Gods, but it is an ominous image, suggestive of an approaching storm. As the hyphenated epithets suggest, Achilles defines himself through destructive action and with its proliferation of phonetically related participles the passage is unlike anything that Coffey had ever written before. The lines which narrate Achilles' violence are tightly organised into recurring patterns of three: three epithets comprise line 5; the three objects of the particple 'skewering' in line 4 establish the pattern; the two caesurae in the following line divide it into three discrete phrases; there are three infinitives in line 8, and so on. An impression of untrammelled violence is suggested by the way the utterance seems to generate its own dynamic. The description of Achilles gives way to a narrative of his actions which proceeds seamlessly into a brief history of the weapon which is used in the performance of these actions. The broad structure of this extended syntactic unit is chiastic: from the history of the spear the lines revert to descriptive participles which in turn give way to another description of the protagonist. Wrenching rhythms and emphatic trochees convey Achilles' murderous energy ('tossing from it corpses to river Xanthus choking it') and they are in stark contrast to the vast, cyclical rhythms through which nature has created an environment capable of nurturing life: 'rise and fall of sea-line to and fro of salt waves' (*DH 5*).

Achilles' heroism, then, is literally and metaphorically an assault on nature itself. The devastating irony of the enjambment 'action man galore/ of slaughter' enables a swift transition into a tonality of forthright condemnation. 'Glory' is denied any positive value and the detached phrases that cut into the line are felt as a series of after-shocks, each one separated by an appalled silence. The values that underpin the heroic ideology, an ideology which would have us understand Achilles as a paragon of human achievement, are revealed to be radically anti-human. As Coffey would have it, 'Prudent Homer' did not endorse these values, and this interpretation of the *Iliad* is not as eccentric as we might think.[20] Michael Silk argues that the *Iliad*, through the character of Achilles, 'subvert(s) the dominant ideological categories that it purports to, and does indeed also, embody'.

A special feature of the poem, that which distinguishes it from *Advent*, is the ease and the economy with which it establishes connections and parallels. In *Advent IV*, for example, the speculative question that prepares the reader for the 'unkin others' is arrived at by way of a particularly unconvincing progression. The mere mention of Cuchulainn in *Death of Hektor* implicates successive generations of Irish heroes and writers – particularly Yeats – at a single touch. A later reference suggests that the ideology of Irish nationalism, as articulated by figures like Pearse, had more in common with Victorian ideology than it might care to admit. The correct placement of individual parts allows the argument to advance swiftly and expand its range of applicability. One does not have to strain to hear the sounds and rhythms of page 7 recurring in page 8. The mind-less complacency of modern society echoes Achilles' mindless violence; ultimately, they both lead to the same results ('limbs corrupted bellies swollen'). The ease with which we happily accommodate the brutality of the Greeks is somehow bound up with our unquestioning conformity to an ideology that promotes greed and exploitation.

While pages 6–8 interweave passages of narrative based on the events in Book XXI with telling commentaries on our interpretation of such narratives, page 10 eliminates commentary and simply focuses on the deception of Hektor and on the litany of mutilations inflicted upon his corpse as they are recorded in Book XXII.

And we are forced to see godlike Achilles with aiding gods
induce Hektor to the test he is doomed to fail
*and* Achilles sent his pierced foe to darkness with jeering words
promising his corpse would be food for dogs and fowl
promising absence of due burial unremittable disgrace
*and* Hektor dead the pallid Greeks draw near
to stab a once feared foe          Then piercing ankles and threading thong
through Achilles fixed corpse to chariot head to trail on ground
*and* mounting beast hero scourged beast as if to flight
*and* making a whirlwind of dust around them as it drew
*and* the dust filled and knotted Hektor's black-brown curls
which sight all Troy with father mother wife mourn to see


Glory for Achilles     Glory for Greeks     Hektor dishonoured

(*DH* 10)

A terrible irony permeates this page. These are scenes that every reader of the *Iliad* is 'forced to see' but, despite his evident bestiality, the representation of Achilles as the quintessential hero persists. I referred to this stanza as a narrative, yet the insistent anaphora really gives it the quality of a list which implicates the reader in an unusual way. There are no pauses because there is nothing to discern and dramatic effect is not sought as an end in itself. The longer line enables Coffey to spell out clearly each outrage and the repeated conjunction controls the tonality because behind each '*and*' can be heard an unspoken 'we are forced to see'. Tenses shift between past and present in a way that makes reading a moral and a political act. The millennia that separate us from the events in Troy are alternately collapsed and re-established so that our perspective is simultaneously that of the silent witness and that of the neutral reader. Our failure to respond correctly, to testify to the truth of what we are forced to see, is set against the response of the Trojans who 'mourn to see' the mutilation of Hektor's corpse.

The temporal scheme of the poem parallels its ternary form. The first five pages move across expanses of time and anticipate a drama that has yet to be enacted; the site of Troy is figured as an empty stage, 'the place of not yet'. Pages 6–10 cast the reader as a spectator in Troy and describe a past event as if it were a drama enacted in the present. The last five pages reflect back on that event and tenses situate Troy firmly in the past: 'Hektor's Troy became a dusty hill swept by cold winds' (*DH* 11). After so much preparation, during which our assumptions about the *Iliad* are unsettled and the respective truth values of history and poetry are objectified to the point where we can evaluate and revise them, the final pages turn to address the question which opened the poem.

The sounds and images that close page 10 ('And/ Doom now in the air like a cloudy mushroom swags above Troy') colour the tonality of the next pages.[21] 'Doom' describes a terrible fate that could equally befall us three millennia later. Yet, as *Death of Hektor* clearly shows, doom can only be enacted as long as the human spirit remains impassive and unawakened. 'Doom' resonates down through pages 11 and 12, and denies any comforting fiction to Hektor and the other Trojans. A crucial ambiguity invites us to reconsider the significance of Hektor by setting his values against ours:

> He'd known no prayer pray cry-mercy-hoped-for prayers
> what we have forgotten and mock at
> he understood the honour due to a hero's corpse
> sought how to soften peace-terms from stronger foe
>
> (*DH* 12)

This capitalised grouping makes up a single statement, but is the second line in apposition to the one before or after it? We may, of course, have forgotten the importance of prayer and the values that a prayerful attitude presupposes, yet the enjambed sense of line 2 conveys another related meaning: Hektor's belief in some higher code remains intact; he, at least, understood what 'we have forgotten and mock at' – the honour due to a hero's corpse.

Hektor submitted himself to 'Doom' and it is a test of our values whether his plea for 'befittingness' redeems him. Our response to his plea serves as an index of our spiritual state as it did for the Greeks and, as *Death of Hektor* argues, the spiritual state of a people will manifest itself in historical change. 'Doom' and negation echo across the stanzas that comprise pages 11 and 12 yet they do not determine the tone of the concluding pages. Hektor's plea, amplified by way of echo through page 13, supersedes 'Doom' and is now offered as a new point of reference for a revised understanding of the *Iliad*, which it became for Coffey himself. The poet's recollected experience of reading the epic provides a smooth transition into the concluding homage to Homer. The visual layout of the last two pages is significant and it bears decisively on the tone of the whole poem. Unlike any of the other pages, the text on it does not rest on the bottom of page 15 and it is significant that it fills a central space that signified silence in previous parts. Homer has left us an important legacy: his Andromache. Her suffering cannot be heard above the clamour of heroic acts; however, it inheres in the silence of the *Iliad* as the 'word hidden for all'. The blocks of text that make up pages 14 and 15 visually describe an ascent and here we remember the image of Homer's words 'surfacing coherent truer than history all and everything' (*DH* 6).

*    *    *

Coffey's *Death of Hektor* stands in a similar relation to the *Iliad* as his translations do to the original poems. Significant resonances and tensions that make the *Iliad* a work of universal relevance are selected and amplified, and inferences are made about values not explicitly asserted in the earlier text. For example, the murder of Astyanax, which is presented as an assumed fact in page 12, is expressed only as the intention of the Greeks in Book XXIII. Such liberties must be understood in the context of the way Coffey's translations of Nerval develop and emphasise possibilities latent in the syntax of a poem like 'El Desdichado'. Tensions inherent in the theology of the *Iliad* – tensions which ought to prompt questions like 'What is the the the role of Fate (*Moira*)?' and 'Is Fate more powerful than Zeus? – are highlighted in page 8 to show that there is sufficient complexity in the epic to unsetttle any assumptions we may make about Homer's beliefs and values. The strategy of selective emphasis by which *Dice Thrown Never Will Annul Chance* gives prominence to positive meanings which are subordinated to a prevailing negative principle in *Un Coup de dés*, is analogous to the way *Death of Hektor* highlights the heroism of the Trojan at the expense of Achilles.

To argue that Hektor is also guilty of acts of brutality or that certain passages in the *Iliad* portray Achilles as a noble figure would be to miss the point and the subtlety of the poem. Coffey's tactic is that of the deconstructive critic: he embarrasses the dominant mode of interpretation by turning the logic of its discourse back on itself. In its moral argument, *Death of Hektor* is no less guilty than traditional interpretations of the *Iliad* in the way that certain possibilities are suppressed and intractable contradictions are glossed over. The poem is certainly tendentious. Yet, by way of moral indignation and celebration, it avows those values in whose name these strategies are deployed thereby calling to account the values that inform those equally biased interpretations which proceed on the assumption that Achilles is the central hero of the *Iliad*.

It is too early to predict how posterity will assess these long poems and one suspects that they will never be admitted into the canon of Irish writing as long as critics continue to evaluate poems in a way that relegates the issue of aesthetic merit. The great paradox here is that *Advent* and *Death of Hektor* have pertinent and discomfiting things to say about Ireland's political and cultural history. One can only suggest that a radical change will have to take place in the landscape of Irish culture before such a dissenting voice will be listened to: only when we begin by listening to *how* this voice articulates its various arguments will we really begin the business of meaningful assessment.

# Appendix

# SYMBOLIC SIGNIFICANCE OF SOUNDS IN *THIRD PERSON*

I base these suggested meanings on the consistency with which particular sounds appear in certain related words and also on their tonal quality. Absolute consistency is impossible. Like Mallarmé, Coffey had to work in a medium that was already formed.

*e* – a bright vowel: consistently sounded in words that present images of nature: *tree, reeds, fields, cedar, weeds, lily, green, leaves, sea, seal*.

*i* – another bright vowel: features in words associated with the eyes and light, the medium of sight : *eyes, crying, blind, light, sign, fire, sky*.

*k* – a hard consonant: associated with shipwreck and demise, darkness and destructive impulses: *wreck, sink, barque, rock, hook, break, broken, black, dark, covered, closed, mask, secret, coal, maledictive*.

*st* – fixity and immobility. Mallarmé wrote: 'La signification fondementale de fixité, et de stationnement, exprimée admirablement par la combinaison *st* . . .'.[1] As this list would suggest, the sound seems to have possessed a similar meaning for Coffey: *stone, standing, stars, constraint, constrained*.

*n* – negation and privation: *no, nothing, never, not, unsaid, unquiet*.

---

[1]  See Robert Greer Cohn, *Towards the Poems of Mallarmé* (Berkeley and Los Angeles: U of California P, 1980), p. 279.

# NOTES

## 1 INTRODUCTION: SOMATIC RHYTHMS

1 'Coffey Answers Questions on Poetry' in Parkman Howe, 'Time and Place: The Poetry and Prose of Brian Coffey' (PhD thesis, University College Dublin, 1982), pp. 272–84 (p. 279).

2 Samuel Beckett, 'On Endgame', *Disjecta: Miscellaneous Writings and a Dramatic Fragment*, ed. Ruby Cohn (London: John Calder, 1983), pp. 106–10 (p. 109).

3 See J.C.C. Mays's preface to Brian Coffey, *Poems and Versions: 1929–1990* (Dublin: Dedalus, 1991), pp. 5–7 (p. 7).

4 Beckett, 'Recent Irish Poetry', *Disjecta*, pp. 70–6 (p. 75).

5 Michael Smith, 'Interview with Mervyn Wall about the Thirties', *The Lace Curtain*, 4 (Summer 1971), pp. 77–86 (p. 82).

6 Howe, 'Coffey Answers Questions on Poetry', p. 274.

7 Brian Coffey, 'A Note on Rat Island', *University Review*, 3.8 (1966), pp. 25–8 (pp. 25–6).

8 Ibid., p. 28. Declan Kiberd makes the same point in his discussion of Yeats's early style: 'Many of Yeats's lyrics are written to a "traditional air" as if the style preceded their content; . . . the poetry evolv[es] more at the instigation of words and rhythms than from the pressure of felt experience.' *Inventing Ireland* (London: Jonathan Cape, 1995), p. 306.

9 Patrick Kavanagh, 'From Monaghan to the Grand Canal' in *Collected Pruse* (London: MacGibbon & Kee, 1967), pp. 223–31 (p. 225).

10 Beckett, 'Recent Irish Poetry', p. 73.

11 Brian Coffey, 'Extracts from "Concerning Making"', *The Lace Curtain*, 6 (Autumn 1978), p. 34.

12 Samuel Beckett, *Collected Poems in English and French* (New York: Grove Press, 1977), p.18.

13 I am referring to the earlier version of 'Spain 1937' which looks forward to a brave new world of socialism in Spain after the Civil War.

14 Denis Devlin, *Collected Poems*, ed. J.C.C. Mays (Dublin: Dedalus, 1989), p. 81.

15 One thinks of Ezra Pound's remarks in his preface to George Oppen's *Discrete Series*: 'I see the difference between the writing of Mr Oppen and Dr Williams, I do not expect any great horde of readers to notice it. They will

perhaps concentrate, or no, they will not concentrate, they will coagulate their rather gelatinous attention on the likeness.' Quoted in Marjorie Perloff, *The Dance of the Intellect: Studies in the Poetry of the Pound Tradition* (Evanston, Illinois: Northwestern UP, 1985), p. 119 *var.*

16  Beckett, 'Homage to Jack B. Yeats', *Disjecta*, p. 149.

17  Kiberd, *Inventing Ireland*, p. 345.

18  Other eminent translators like Ezra Pound, Walter Benjamin, Octavia Paz and Vladimir Nabokov, in their different ways, worked outside the dominant Anglo-American paradigm. Benjamin, for example, wrote: 'it is not the highest praise of a translation, particularly in the age of its origin, to say that it reads as if it had been originally written in that language'. See 'The Task of the Translator' in Marcus Bullock and Michael W. Jennings (eds), *Walter Benjamin: Selected Writings Volume I* (Cambridge, Mass., and London: Harvard UP, 1996), p. 260.

19  For a comparable treatment of a similar kind of writing see 'Zukofsky and Mallarmé: Notes on "A"–19', Kenneth Cox's illuminating analysis of Louis Zukofsky's incorporation of Mallarmé's 'Le Guignon' into 'A'–19, *Maps # 5*, 1973, pp. 1–11.

20  Quoted in S.B. Kennedy, *Irish Art and Modernism 1880–1950* (Belfast: Institute of Irish Studies, 1991), p. 36.

21  T.S. Eliot, '*Ulysses*, Order and Myth', *The Dial*, LXXV (Nov. 1923), 480–3; Reprinted in Robert A. Deming (ed.), *James Joyce:The Critical Heritage* (London: Routledge & Kegan Paul, 2 vols, 1970), Vol. I, pp. 268–71 (p. 270).

22  Coffey believed that the poet's use of language was antithetical to the politician's and the propagandist's. 'Propagandists and politicals use words like counters, bits and pieces to be moved about the surface of the original draft of a speech, say; for poets a word partakes as much of the bodily conditions of moving breath and unconscious mimetic reflexes of one's body in speech, as of all that emanates from the *heart*', Brian Coffey 'Extracts from "Concerning Making"', *The Lace Curtain*, 6 (Autumn 1978), 32.

23  Alex Davis, '"Poetry is Ontology": Brian Coffey's Poetics' in Patricia Coughlan and Alex Davis (eds), *Modernism and Ireland: The Poetry of the 1930s* (Cork: Cork UP, 1995), pp. 150–72.

## 2 THIRD PERSON (1938)

1  *Times Literary Supplement*, 3 September 1938, p. 574

2  In a letter to Thomas MacGreevy, 27 October 1936, Coffey included Valéry's theoretical books in a list of sources he intended to work into an essay about the origins of poetic inspiration. (TCD MS 8110/ 23). W.N. Ince discusses this aspect of Valéry's thought in *The Poetic Theory of Paul Valery: Inspiration and Technique* (Leicester: Leicester UP, 1970), pp. 77–94.

3  Samuel Beckett, *Texts For Nothing* (London: Calder & Boyars, 1974), p. 22.

4  For 'he' read also 'she' and 'they'. The same applies for corresponding possesive pronouns and adjectives.

5  See Coffey's letter to Thomas MacGreevy, 14 May 1934 (TCD MS 8110/10).

6  'Brian Coffey, An Interview by Parkman Howe', *Éire/Ireland*, 13.1 (1978), pp. 113–23 (p. 121).

 7 The abbreviation, *PV*, will be used hereafter to refer to Brian Coffey, *Poems and Versions 1929–1990*.

 8 'Brian Coffey, An Interview', p. 121.

 9 Brian Coffey, 'Of Denis Devlin: Vestiges, Sentences, Presages', *University Review*, 2.11 (1961), pp. 3–18 (p. 12).

10 Paul Eluard, *Oeuvres Complètes I* (Paris: Gallimard, 1968), p. 238.

11 This stanza shows the importance of Eliot as an influence. The syntax bears a striking resemblance to that of *Ash-Wednesday* (1930), which opens thus: 'Because I do not hope to turn again/ Because I do not hope/ Because I do not hope to turn/ . . .'.

12 A comparison with an earlier draft of the poem shows how Coffey worked to 'tweak up' his synthesis. He obviously intended some elemental synthesis. The more prosaic 'wind' does not have the same point as 'sun' however. (TCD MS 8110/ 21).

> Where fountains danced once in the wind
> The owl starts his evening flight . . .

13 MacLeish's sonnet ends with the lines: 'There in the sudden blackness the black pall/ Of nothing, nothing, nothing – nothing at all.' See Geoffrey Moore ed., *The Penguin Book of American Verse* (Harmondsworth: Penguin, 1989), p. 325.

14 Paul Eluard, *Oeuvres Complètes I*, p. 493.

15 J.G. Fichte, 'Some Lectures Concerning the Scholar's Vocation', trans. David Breazeale, in Rüdiger Bubner (ed.), *German Idealist Philosophy* (Harmondsworth: Penguin, 1997), pp. 121–59 (p. 136). The italics are the author's.

16 Karlheinz Stierle,'Position and Negation in Mallarmé's "Prose pour des Esseintes"', *Yale French Studies*, 54 (1978), pp. 96–117 (p. 102).

17 Parkman Howe, 'Time and Place', p. 72.

18 James Knowlson, *Damned to Fame: The Life of Samuel Beckett* (London: Bloomsbury, 1996), p. 181. Knowlson writes: 'Beckett [in the opinion of Bion] had to learn to counter his self-immersion by coming out of himself more in his daily life and taking a livelier interest in others. . . Yet the evidence of his friends suggests that what may once have been a search for a tolerable *modus vivendi* evolved into a far more natural, spontaneous sharing in the problems, pains and sufferings of others'. Coffey wrote that Celia, from *Murphy*, 'is the door of entry to the world of Beckett's compassion, which is not to be traced back to some nexus of literary influences.' See Brian Coffey, 'Memory's Murphy Maker: Some Notes on Samuel Beckett', *Threshold*, 17 (1962), pp. 26–36 (p. 32).

19 In Christian symbolism, the red rose is a symbol of martyrdom, while the white rose is a symbol of purity. Dawn symbolises the blood and the Advent of Christ. See George Ferguson, *Signs and Symbols in Christian Art* (New York: Oxford UP, 1954), pp. 47 and 54.

20 Brian Coffey, 'A Note on Rat Island', p. 27.

21 Steven Connor, *Samuel Beckett: Repetition, Theory and Text* (Oxford: Blackwell, 1988), p. 15.

22 Coffey once wrote that Hyde's – and presumably by implication any other poet's – attempts to imitate in English the rhythmic, rhyming and alliterative schemes of Gaelic would 'cure any poet-reader of Saintsbury's history of

English prosody. . . from any attempt to work right against the tradition and the spirit of English verse.' See Coffey, 'Of Denis Devlin', p. 11.

23 Clarke apparently gave *Third Person* a negative review in his weekly poetry programme for Radio Éireann. The review has been lost. Denis Donoghue's remarks concerning Clarke's lack of interest in the programme, which was evident in its 'disgracefully slack' reviews, suggest that Clarke would not have been favourably disposed to a work as challenging as *Third Person*. See Denis Donoghue, *We Irish: Essays on Irish Literature and Society* (Berkeley and Los Angeles: U of California P, 1986), pp. 244–5.

24 These lines almost read like an address to the reader in which case he/she is 'reflected' in what is, after all, a remarkably fluid text. There is textual evidence to suggest that this could well be the case. In a letter to MacGreevy, 15 December 1936 (TCD MS 8110/24), in which he discusses Denis Devlin's writing habits Coffey comments on his (Devlin's) refusal 'to leave a rhythm alone'. This is immediately preceded by a main clause that reads: 'All his out flies [*sic*] calms the temptations of any dragon-fly: . . .'. The sense is obscure but a mutual understanding of the significance of 'dragon-fly' is implied. Whatever meaning was intended, the 'dragon-fly' seems to possess something like a symbolic significance within the context of reading or writing poetry.

25 Stephen Mitchell translates the lines thus: 'Let us lament together that someone pulled you/ out of your mirror's depths.' *The Selected Poetry of Rainer Maria Rilke* (London: Picador, 1987) p. 79. Rilke identified aesthetic contemplation with the idea of perfect mirroring.

26 Commenting on Beckett's early collection *Echo's Bones*, Coffey praised its author's ability to hear 'the clarity of vowels'. Brian Coffey 'Memory's Murphy Maker', p. 31.

27 See Robert Gibson (ed.), *Modern French Poets on Poetry* (Cambridge: Cambridge UP, 1961). Mallarmé wrote: 'Le Mot présente, dans ses voyelles et ses diphtongues, comme une chair; et dans ses consonnes, comme une ossature délicate à disséquer.' (p. 157).

28 J. Patrick Byrne, 'Assonance and Modern Irish Poetry', *Dublin Magazine*, 13.3 (July–Sept. 1938), 52–62.

29 Ibid., 61.

30 It could just as easily be argued that Higgins's use of assonance gives his verse a distinctly English sound. I am thinking particularly of pre-Romantic poets like William Cowper. Cowper addresses Evening as follows:

> Come, Evening once again, season of peace,
> Return, sweet Evening, and continue long!
> Methinks I see thee in the streaky west,
> With matron-step . . .

(*The Task*, Bk IV lines 243–6)

31 The *First Book of Odes* was first published in *Redimiculum Matellarum* in 1930 and *Chomei at Toyama* in *Poetry* (Chicago) Vol. 42, Sept. 1933. Both are now collected in Basil Bunting, *Collected Poems* (Oxford: Oxford UP, 1978), pp. 75 and 68.

32 'Dedication' may have evolved out of a translation of Eluard's 'Par Une Nuit Nouvelle', whose opening lines echo a relative pronoun and move methodically

through repeated phrases which are differentiated only by inflections of tense much like the short stanzas of Coffey's poem. See Paul Eluard, *Oeuvres Complètes I*, p. 366. The lyric opens with the following lines:

> Femme avec laquelle j'ai vécu
> Femme avec laquelle je vis
> Femme avec laquelle je vivrai
> Toujours la même

33 Brian Coffey, 'Denis Devlin: Poet of Distance' in Andrew Carpenter (ed.), *Place, Personality and the Irish Writer* (Gerrards Cross: Colin Smythe, 1977), pp. 137–57 (p. 145 specifically).

34 I read 'when' as an unstressed syllable.

35 Note how Coffey improves upon this early version of 'Content', which he sent to MacGreevy in 1935 (TCD MS 8110/20), by simply substituting 'night' for the rather limp '. . . that move/ Faster than I can count': 'From the womb/ To the Grave/ Seventy years that move/ Faster than I can count'. Incidentally, the earlier version includes an epigraph, 'Playing songs to empty pockets' – again, a fortunate revision.

36 This subject is treated in J.C.C. Mays, 'Introduction', *Collected Poems of Denis Devlin* (Dublin: Dedalus, 1989), pp. 22–45.

37 George Oppen, *Discrete Series* in Andrew McAllister (ed.), *The Objectivists* (Newcastle: Bloodaxe, 1996), p. 43 var. All subsequent references to *Discrete Series* can be found in this volume.

38 'Amaranth' presents one instance of this kind of difficulty, i.e. 'santonine your sign'. Santonine is an extract from the santonica plant, otherwise known as wormwood. It is a very bitter substance, from which I infer that the speaker is passing comment on the bitterness or spite of the auditor.

39 L.S. Dembo, 'Interview with George Oppen', *Contemporary Literature*, 10.2 (Spring 1969), pp. 159–77 (p. 161).

40 The reference is to 'Party on Shipboard' from *Discrete Series*, p. 51.

41 The phrase comes from Oppen's 'Statement on Poetics' in Charles Tomlinson (ed.), *Poems of George Oppen* (Newcastle: Cloud, 1990), p. 61.

42 *Discrete Series*, p. 43 var.

43 Oppen gave his Objectivist aesthetic another twist by sometimes arranging poems visually to form the shapes of the objects he describes, see 'The three wide/ Funnels . . .', *Discrete Series* p. 45. Coffey's later pattern poems form symbols rather than objects much like the pattern poems of George Herbert.

44 The phrase is from 'Four Quartets: East Coker', *The Complete Poems and Plays* (London: Faber & Faber, 1989), p. 182.

45 John Hollander, *The Figure of Echo: A Mode of Allusion in Milton and After* (Berkeley: U of California P, 1981), p. 64 and passim.

46 *Poems of Sir Samuel Ferguson*, (Dublin: Talbot Press, 1918), p. 2. The line is from the fourth stanza of 'The Burial of King Cormac':

> They loosed their curse against the king;
>     They cursed him in his flesh and bones;
> And daily in their mystic ring
>     They turn'd the maledictive stones,

The scenes depicted on the citizen's facecloth or 'emunctory field' in Episode 12 of *Ulysses* include '. . . cromlechs and grianauns and seats of learning and maledictive stones. . .'. See James Joyce, *Ulysses* (London: The Bodley Head, 1949), p. 316.

47 'Spurred' includes the lines 'Those you clutch at/ are eyes you dare not see' which seem to consciously allude to the following lines from 'The Hollow Men': 'Eyes I dare not meet in dreams/ In death's dream kingdom/. . .' The lines 'I give you to learn/ broken stems ice wind/ that you who live are dead' from 'Gentle' could allude to 'I could not/ Speak, and my eyes failed, I was neither/ Living nor dead, . . . ' from *The Waste Land*: 'The Burial of the Dead'. I suggest Coffey is making an allusion because like Eliot's poem, 'Gentle' expresses an inner state in terms of a failure to see. The surrounding contexts of both lines is also similar because both feature a presentation of emblematic flowers; hyacinths in Eliot's case, laurels, thorns and broken stems in Coffey's.

48 TCD MS 8110/23 27 October 1936.

49 Dante Alighieri, *La Divina Commedia*, Vol. II, *Purgatorio*, Natalino Sapegno ed. (Firenze: Le Nuova Italia Editrice, 1969) p. 206. The quotation is from Canto XIX, lines 19–21.

50 See *A Catholic Dictionary* (London: Kegan Paul, Trench, Trübner & Co., 1903) p. 904.

51 This is a paraphrase, albeit simplified, of notes Coleridge had inscribed in his copy of one of Schelling's volumes. The fragment is printed in Mary Anne Perkins, *Coleridge's Philosophy: The Logos as Unifying Principle* (Oxford: Clarendon, 1994). The quotation, which is from a manuscript entitled 'On the Divine Ideas' can be found on p. 193.

52 Ibid. pp. 252–4. Coleridge does not intend 'negative' to be understood as '*nihilative*, . . . mere privation'. It should be interpreted as 'the correspondent Opposite of the Power first *put*.'

53 See Thomas MacGreevy, *Collected Poems*, ed. Susan Schreibman (Dublin: Anna Livia, 1991) p. 25

54 See Mays, Preface, Coffey, *Poems and Versions*, p. 5.

55 Jack Yeats's novel *The Amaranthers* (1936), which tells of a journey to an enchanted island off the west of Ireland, is another probable allusion.

56 M.L. Rosenthal and Sally M. Gall, *The Modern Poetic Sequence: The Genius of Modern Poetry* (Oxford and New York: Oxford UP, 1983), p. 9.

57 Earl Miner, 'Some Issues for Study of Integrated Collections' in Neil Fraistat (ed.), *Poems in Their Place: The Intertextuality and Order of Poetic Collections* (Chapel Hill: U of North Carolina P, 1986), pp. 18–43 (p. 31).

58 Mark Jeffreys, 'Ideologies of Lyric: A Problem of Genre in Contemporary Anglophone Poetics', *PMLA*, 110.2 (1995), pp. 196–205 (p. 203).


## 3 COFFEY'S METHOD OF TRANSLATION

1 Vladimir Nabokov, 'Problems of Translation: *Onegin* in English' in Rainer Schulte and John Biguenet (eds), *Theories of Translation: An Anthology of Essays from Dryden to Derrida* (Chicago and London: U of Chicago P: 1992), pp. 127–43 (p. 135).

2 Throughout this chapter I use the phrase 'deviant translation' to identify Coffey's peculiar mode of critique. Philip E. Lewis uses the term 'abusive translation'. Although he makes no reference to Coffey, Lewis's understanding of this phrase perfectly describes Coffey's strategy. 'Abusive translation', he writes, has the effect of 'directing a critical thrust back toward the text that it translates and in relation to which it becomes a kind of unsettling aftermath (it is as if the translation sought to occupy the original's already unsettled home, and thereby, far from 'domesticating' it, to turn it into a place still more foreign to itself). See Philip E. Lewis, 'The Measure of Translation Effects' in Joseph Graham (ed.), *Difference in Translation* (Ithaca: Cornell UP, 1985), pp. 31–62 (p. 43).

3 See Coffey's letter to MacGreevy, 28 October 1933 (TCD MS 8110/4).

4 Arthur Rimbaud, *Oeuvres Complètes* (Paris: Gallimard, 1972), pp. 66–9 (p. 66).

5 Beckett, *Collected Poems in English and French*, pp. 92–105 (p. 93).

6 See Gibson, *Modern French Poets on Poetry*, p. 94.

7 Brian Coffey, trans. 'The Joy-Mad Ship', by Arthur Rimbaud, *Irish University Review*, 5.1 (Spring 1975), pp. 75–8 (p. 75).

8 Rimbaud, *Oeuvres Complètes*, p. 249. The italics are the author's.

9 Derek Mahon, 'from "The Druken Boat"', *Selected Poems* (London: Viking/Gallery/Oxford UP, 1991), pp. 80–1 (p. 81).

10 Later, in *Une Saison en Enfer*, a disillusioned Rimbaud mocked as one of his youthful 'folies' a yearning for an idealised personal and historical past: 'Depuis longtemps, . . . [je] . . . trouvais dérisoires les célébrités de la peinture et de la poésie moderne . . . J'aimais . . . la littérature démodée, latin d'église, livres érotiques sans orthographe, romans de nos aïeules; contes de fées, petits livres de l'enfance . . .'. See *Oeuvres Complètes*, p. 106.

11 Marshall Lindsay, 'Poetic Doctrine in Three of Rimbaud's Verse Poems' in *Rimbaud: Modern Critical Views*, ed. Harold Bloom (New York: Chelsea House, 1988), pp. 129–43 (p. 138).

12 Perhaps the yearning of the boat for the 'black pool'– 'dubh linn' in Irish – possessed a particular resonance for Coffey.

13 Lindsay, 'Poetic Doctrine', p. 138.

14 He has also managed to capture the sudden shift to quiet lyricism in the penultimate stanza by matching Rimbaud's carefully modulated rhythms.

15 The stripping away of the glamorous trappings of warfare in order to expose the human suffering that they concealed was a central concern in *Death of Hektor*.

16 'Pontons' were nineteenth-century prison boats. 'Hulks' catches this meaning.

17 The verb also has a phonetic association with 'scrutinise', which is etymologically related to the Latin verb *scrutari*, 'to search'.

18 Brian Coffey, 'El Desdichado' by Gérard de Nerval, *Irish University Review*, 5.1 (Spring 1975), p. 73. Coffey's revised version of 'El Desdichado' and his translations of the other sonnets that comprise Nerval's sequence can be found in *The Poet's Voice*, 3.3 (1987), pp. 31–5. For an altogether more reliable text of these translations one should consult a recent reprint in *etruscan reader* VII, 1997, pp. 107–16. My discussion of Coffey's translations is based on this text, unless otherwise stated.

19  In her exegetical text *Gérard de Nerval: Les Chimères* (Geneva: Droz, 1969), Jeanine Moulin writes 'Avec El Desdichado, l'éloquence de la poésie française subit une première et rude atteinte', p. 10.
20  Derek Mahon, *The Chimeras* (Dublin: Gallery, 1982), p. 9.
21  Robin Blaser's translation of *Les Chimères* was first published in *Caterpillar* 12, July 1970, pp. 2–14.
22  Gérard de Nerval, *Oeuvres Complètes III* (Paris: Gallimard, 1993), p. 645.
23  Jacques Dhaenens, *Le destin d'Orphée: 'El Desdichado' de Nerval* (Paris: Librairie Minard, 1972), p. 40. Dhaenens quotes a passage from Nerval's *Les Illuminés* which suggests that Nerval was quick to spot contradictory feelings in others. In a passage describing the character of Restif de la Bretonne Nerval writes: 'Il était, – selon son expression même, – consolé par le désespoir', p. 41.
24  Octave Nadal, 'Poetique et Poésie des *Chimères*', *Mercure de France*, 325 (Nov. 1955), p. 410. It is highly probable that Coffey, who prepared scrupulously for each set of translations, had read Octave Nadal's important study of *Les Chimères* before revising 'El Desdichado'. Discussing the meaning of this line, Nadal writes: 'Mais dans l'abîme, au coeur de l'ombre, au fond de la pierre et de la matière la plus inerte, demeure une espérance. Nerval garde le souvenir de l'être, la nostalgie de la lumière, de la voix et du regard qui détruit la mort. "Dans la nuit du tombeau toi qui m'as consolé."' Note the omission of the comma.
25  This close identification of the muse with the emblematic flower recurs in 'Artemis', the fourth sonnet of the sequence.
26  Dhaenens, *Le Destin d'Orphée*, p. 44.
27  The need to resolve the conflicting demands of familial duty and poetry was a moral issue for Coffey. It was an important theme in *Missouri Sequence*.
28  J.C.C. Mays, 'Brian Coffey's Work in Progress', *Krino*, 4 (Autumn 1987), p. 65.
29  Mahon, *The Chimeras*, p.9.
30  Sidney B. Smith, Review of Derek Mahon's *The Chimeras*, *Poetry Ireland*, 7 (Spring–Summer 1983), 47–8. The 'smoothness' and polished elegance of Mahon's versions preclude any real examination of the tension between Nerval's formal classicism and his more mercurial turns of thought. The profusion of Mediterranean light and the sense of natural abundance in the opening stanza of 'Myrtho', for example, are carefully domesticated in Mahon's translation. Tellingly, Mahon's version contains a faint allusion to Kubla Khan's 'sunny dome'.

| Myrtho, dark sorceress, I think of you; | I muse on you, Myrtho, godlike enchantress, |
| Of high Posilipo – that dome of fire – | Posilipo lofty, a glitter a thousand fires, |
| Your features sculpted to an orient glow, | your brow flooded by lucent Orient, |
| The black grapes clustered in your golden hair. | and black grapes tangled with your gold braids. |
| [Mahon] | [Coffey] |

Coffey's translation of Nerval's verbs 'inondé' and 'mêlés' as 'flooded' and 'tangled' respectively, and the image in line 2 are crucial because they give point to the synthesis of luxuriant paganism and pallid Christianity that concludes the poem: 'Le pâle Hortensia s'unit au Myrthe vert!' Note also how Coffey retains the important fusion of light and liquid in line 3.

31  Brian Coffey, *Poems and Versions*, pp. 117–21.

32  It is also possible that Coffey's translation of the last sonnet in *Les Chimères*, 'Vers dorés', which comments ironically on man's alienation from the natural world, prompted a deeper appreciation of the complexities of 'El Desdichado'.

33  Burton Hatlen, 'Catullus Metamorphosed', *Paideuma*, 7.3 (Winter 1978), pp. 539–45 (p. 542). Hatlen writes: 'Anyone who has ever seen an erect penis knows that it is a "bow" in at least three senses: it curves like a bow, it is aimed at an object of desire, and it is ready to shoot'.

34  Lawrence Venuti, *The Translator's Invisibility: A History of Translation* (London and New York: Routledge, 1995), p. 216.

35  Nerval, *Oeuvres Complètes III*, p. 651.

36  Brian Coffey, *The Chimeras*, p. 116.

37  Coffey, *Poems and Versions*, pp. 149, 148.

38  It is also worth noting Coffey's refusal to capitalise Nerval's 'Dieu caché' in line 12 of his translation.

39  See Blaser's short manifesto 'The Fire', printed in *Caterpillar*, 12 (July 1970), pp. 15–23 (p. 15).

40  Blaser's translations of *Les Chimères* also appear in ibid., pp. 2–13.

41  Nerval, *Oeuvres Complètes III*, p. 651.

42  See Blaser's note on his translations, p. 14.

43  Douglas Sealy, Review of *Dice Thrown Never Will Annul Chance* by Brian Coffey, *The Irish Times*, 24 April 1965. Sealy writes: 'The poem is obviously untranslatable, . . . Despite the commentators, I find the poem meaningless, whether in English or French.'

44  A verso and recto side together make up a single opening or spread. Unlike other translations of *Un Coup de dés*, Coffey's *Dice Thrown Never Will Annul Chance* is not paginated. This is in keeping with the format of the original poem. There are eleven openings in all.

45  Stéphane Mallarmé, *Un Coup de dés jamais n'abolira le hasard* in *Oeuvres Complètes*, eds Henri Mondor and G. Jean Aubry (Paris: Gallimard, 1951), opening 6. The abbreviation *CD* will be used hereafter to refer to this work.; 'O' refers to opening numbers.

46  Stéphane Mallarmé, *Collected Poems*, trans. Henry Weinfield (Berkeley, CA: U of California P, 1994) p. 134. Weinfield's is the only commercially available translation of *Un Coup de dés*.

47  Brian Coffey, trans., *Dice Thrown Never Will Annul Chance*, by Stéphane Mallarmé (Dublin: Dolmen, 1965), opening 6. The abbreviation *DT* will be used hereafter to refer to this work.

48  Gardner Davies, *Vers Une Explication Rationelle du Coup de Dés* (Paris: José Corti, 1953), p. 82.

49  Virginia La Charité, *The Dynamics of Space: Mallarmé's 'Un Coup de Dés Jamais N'Abolira le Hasard'* (Lexington, Kentucky: French Forum Publishers, 1987), p. 56.

50  The Larousse Dictionary cites as an example of this usage of 'abolir' Baudelaire's sentence, 'L'âge ne change que la voix, et n'abolit que les cheveux et les dents.'

51  It must be added here that the French verb 'annuler' does not possess the metaphysical flavour of the English 'annul' which is closer in meaning to this specific sense of 'abolir' and 'anéantir'.

52  See Weinfield (trans.), Mallarmé, *Collected Poems*, p. 267.

53  Daisy Aldan's *A Throw Of The Dice Never Will Abolish Chance* (New York: Tiber Press, 1956) was the first translation of *Un Coup de dés* into English. Unlike Coffey she suppresses any trace of positive meaning by adopting the unusual expedient of repeating the negative term 'Never'. Her translation and disposal of the main idea across the poem read as follows: A THROW OF THE DICE/ NEVER/ NEVER WILL ABOLISH/ CHANCE.

54  Mallarmé frequently used the phrase 'symphonic equation' when describing what he hoped his poetry could realise through form. Robert G. Cohn writes that the syntactical form of this line illustrates what Mallarmé meant by the phrase. See Robert G. Cohn, *Mallarmé's Masterwork: New Findings* (The Hague and Paris: Mouton, 1966), p. 79.

55  The italics are mine.

56  Perhaps Coffey might have considered another translation of 'né/ d'un ébat': 'born/ of a gambol'. The obvious pun may struck him as a little crass.

57  One thinks here of Beckett's late fiction the constitutive principle of which is the repeated, almost ritualised, deferral of the inevitable moment.

58  Sealy's comments can be found in the review cited above (note 43). For Howe's brief discussion see 'Time and Place', pp. 168–73 (p. 171).

59  Davies, *Vers Une Explication*, p. 116.

60  Quoted in Venuti, *The Translator's Invisibility*, p. 216.

61  'Tome' was a favourite Mallarméan word because it simultaneously suggested 'book' and 'tomb'.

62  See Anthony Hartley (ed. and trans.), *Mallarmé* (Harmondsworth: Penguin, 1965), p. 221. Hartley's is a plain prose translation.

63  See Weinfield, p.140. Hartley also gives this translation, see p. 229.

64  Brian Coffey, 'Notes on Modern Cosmological Speculation', *The Modern Schoolman*, 29.3 (March 1952), pp. 183–96 (pp. 188, 195).

65  La Charité, *The Dynamics of Space*, pp. 165–6.

66  The sounds and movement of the sea can be heard and felt throughout *Dice Thrown*. The bottom right hand corner of opening 9 features a wonderfully evocative passage: '*Drops/ the quill/ rhythmical suspending of defeat/ to bury itself/ in the original spray/ whence but lately whose frenzy sprang as far as a peak/ blasted/ by the identical neutrality of the gulf*'.

67  Isaiah 53: 12: 'Therefore I will divide him a portion with the great, and he shall divide the spoil with the strong; because he had poured out his soul to death'. Joel 2: 28: 'And it shall come to pass afterward, that I will pour out my spirit on all flesh'.

68  Brian Coffey, 'Introduction', *Poems of Mallarmé: Bilingual Edition* (London and Dublin: New Writers' Press/Menard Press, 1990), p. 5.

69  Yves Bonnefoy, 'The Poetics of Mallarmé', *Yale French Studies*, 54 (1977), pp. 9–21 (p. 10).

70  This passage from *Advent II* seems intended as a riposte to Mallarmé's sonnet:

> It is here in the passing swan beauty beauty swan
> jade on down a flow going past not nothingness

(PV 120)

71 'Plume'(openings 7 and 9), which functions as a symbol of the master's hesitancy in *Un Coup de dés* and which most would translate as 'feather' is rendered as 'quill' by Coffey. He also gives 'in a flash' (*DT*, O.7) for Mallarmé's 'en foudre' while Weinfield gives 'in a lightning flash' (p. 136); Hartley gives 'in thunder' (p. 225).

72 Aldan translates these lines as 'before it halts/ at some point which consecrates it'.

73 Towards the end of *Advent I*, (*PV* 116) Coffey presents a concise paraphrase of Aquinas's third proof of the existence of God, the famous 'Tertia Via' from *Summa Theologiae*. The passage is proleptic: it anticipates future references to Mallarmé's thought and refutes it in advance:

> Think world with you
> think total voiding all whatever naughted and you too
> if once all with us were naught
> could aught ever be

74 It is also possible that Coffey was subtly signifying his resistance to the notion that the only exception to the general argument of the poem was the poem itself by playing on the verb 'to except', which when used intransitively means 'to object to' or 'to take exception to'.

75 It seems worthwhile speculating on the possibility that Coffey was trying to capture some of the sense of 'vertige' by this oblique reference to the Mount of Olives whose summit commanded a spectacular view of Jerusalem and the surrounding territory.

76 Robert G. Cohn, *Mallarmé's 'Un Coup de Dés': An Exegesis* (New Haven: Yale French Studies, 1949), p. 80.

77 Terry Hale, Review of *The Translator's Invisibility* by Lawrence Venuti, *Times Literary Supplement*, 6 September 1996.

## 4 SOUND AND METRICS IN *ADVENT* (1975) AND *DEATH OF HEKTOR* (1982)

1 Anthony Cronin, 'The Poetry of Brian Coffey', *The Irish Times*, 20 February 1976.

2 Hugh Kenner uses the term 'subject-rhymes' in his discussion of Pound's *Cantos*. See Hugh Kenner, *The Pound Era: The Age of Ezra Pound, T.S. Eliot, James Joyce and Wyndham Lewis* (London: Faber & Faber, 1972), p. 365.

3 Brian Coffey, *Death of Hektor* (London: Menard Press, 1982), p. 11. The abbreviation, *DH*, will be used hereafter to refer to this work.

4 Benjamin Hrushovski, 'The Meaning of Sound Patterns in Poetry', *Poetics Today*, 2.1 (1980), pp. 39–56 (p. 51).

5 John Hollander, *The Figure of Echo*. Hollander writes: 'texts themselves in manifesting schematic repetition or self-echo can be particularly resonant when picked up allusively later on', p. 127.

6  Jacques Maritain, *Art and Scholasticism and The Frontiers of Poetry*, trans. Joseph W. Evans (New York: Charles Scribner's Sons, 1962), p. 128.

7  Aristotle, 'On the Art of Poetry' in *Aristotle/ Horace/Longinus: Classical Literary Criticism* trans. T.S. Dorsch (Harmondsworth: Penguin, 1987), pp. 31–75 (pp. 43–4).

8  Coffey's son Dominic adopted the lifestyle of a biker and was fatally injured in a motorcycle accident.

9  It is perhaps significant that Mallarmé was similarly bereaved. His eight-year-old son died of an illness.

10  The reprint of *Death of Hektor* in *Poems and Versions* does not have this visual element.

11  The phrase is, of course, from the opening paragraph of Beckett's *The Unnamable*.

12  Brian Coffey, 'Extracts from "Concerning Making"', p. 36.

13  One thinks here of Eliot's lines in *Ash Wednesday V*:

> Where shall the word be found, where will the word
> Resound? Not here, there is not enough silence.

14  Chapman, who provided the first important versions of Homer in the English language, wrote that while translating the *Iliad*, 'the first free light of my author entred and emboldened me'. The light of his new understanding illuminated the heroism of Hektor. Quoted in Charlotte Spivack's *George Chapman* (New York: Twayne Publishers, 1967), p. 55. Coffey in his 'Concerning Making' writes: 'And the reading of Homer, even if done in the magical englishing Homer undergoes at the hands of Chapman, is more beneficial to poets of the Ireland of today than would be the reading of Yeats', p. 36.

15  Quoted in Kenner, *The Pound Era*, p. 371.

16  Those who might object that this appeal to the 'living voice' reveals a phonocentric prejudice ought to consult Garrett Stewart's *Reading Voices* (Berkeley, Los Angeles and Oxford: U of California P, 1990). Stewart argues that the 'somatic locus of soundless reception includes of course the brain but must be said to encompass as well the organs of vocal production, from diaphragm up through throat to tongue and palate' (p. 1).

17  As the epigraph to chapter one clearly demonstrates, Coffey did not feel obliged to write poems that scanned conveniently into iambs. Indeed, he stressed the primal, somatic origins of his rhythms. Surprisingly, this is an aspect of his poetry that almost everybody has missed.

18  Stewart, *Reading Voices*, p. 5.

19  The quoted phrase is from Joyce's *A Portrait of the Artist as a Young Man* (Harmondsworth: Penguin, 1992), p. 233.

20  See Michael Silk, *Homer: The Iliad* (Cambridge: Cambridge UP, 1987), p. 96. Oliver Taplin comments on the moral complexity of the epic and identifies a recurring debate about values that runs through the many passages of direct speech: 'If the 'Heroic Code' were agreed and beyond dispute, there would be no real conflict', see Oliver Taplin, 'Homer' in *Greece and the Hellenistic World* eds. John Boardman, Jasper Griffin and Oswyn Murray (Oxford: Oxford UP, 1990), pp. 44–71 (p. 68).

21 The word 'swag' is resonant with Blakean associations: 'Hungry clouds swag on the deep' (*The Marriage of Heaven and Hell*, lines 2, 22; see also *Vala, or the Four Zoas* lines 100, 176, 563). 'Swag' appears in *Advent I* also see *PV*, pp. 44–71 (pp. 114–15).

# BIBLIOGRAPHY

Addis, William and Arnold, Thomas. *A Catholic Dictionary*. London: Kegan Paul, Trench, Trübner and Co. Ltd., 1903.

Aldan, Daisy, trans. *A Throw Of The Dice Will Never Abolish Chance*. By Stéphane Mallarmé. New York: Tiber Press, 1956.

Aristotle. 'On the Art of Poetry.' Trans. T.S. Dorsch. In *Aristotle/ Horace/ Longinus: Classical Literary Criticism*. Harmondsworth: Penguin, 1987: 29–75.

Beckett, Samuel. *Collected Poems in English and French*. New York: Grove Press, 1977.

———. *Disjecta: Miscellaneous Writings and a Dramatic Fragment*. Introd. and ed. Ruby Cohn. London: John Calder, 1983.

———. *Texts for Nothing*. London: Calder & Boyars, 1974.

Benjamin, Walter. *Selected Writings: Volume I*. Eds Marcus Bullock and Michael W. Jennings. Cambridge, Mass. and London: Harvard UP, 1996.

Blaser, Robin, trans. *Les Chimères*. By Gérard de Nerval. *Caterpillar 12*, (July 1970): 2–14.

Bonnefoy, Yves. 'The Poetics of Mallarmé.' *Yale French Studies*, 54 (1977): 9–21.

Bowie, Malcolm. *Mallarmé and the Art of Being Difficult*. Cambridge: Cambridge UP, 1978.

Bunting, Basil. *Collected Poems*. Oxford: UP, 1978.

Byrne, J. Patrick. 'Assonance and Modern Irish Poetry.' *The Dublin Magazine*, 13.3 (1938): 52–62.

Coffey, Brian. 'A Note on Rat Island.' *University Review*, 3.8 (1966): 25–8

———, trans. *The Chimeras*. By Gérard de Nerval. *etruscan reader*, VII (1997): 107–16.

———. *Death of Hektor*. London : Menard Press, 1982.

———. 'Denis Devlin: Poet of Distance.' In *Place, Personality and the Irish Writer*. Ed. Andrew Carpenter. Gerrards Cross: Colin Smythe, 1977: 137–57.

———, trans. *Dice Thrown Never Will Annul Chance*. By Stéphane Mallarmé. Dublin: Dolmen, 1965.

———. 'Extracts from "Concerning Making".' *The Lace Curtain*, No. 6 (Autumn 1978) : 31–7.

———. 'Memory's Murphy Maker: Some Notes on Samuel Beckett.' *Threshold*, No. 17 (1962): 28–36.

———— . 'Notes on Modern Cosmological Speculation.' *The Modern Schoolman*, 29.3 (1952): 183–96.

———— . 'Of Denis Devlin: Vestiges, Sentences, Presages.' *University Review*, 2.11 (1961): 3–18.

———— . *Poems and Versions 1929–1990*. Dublin: Dedalus, 1991.

———— , trans. *Poems of Mallarmé: A Bilingual Edition*. London and Dublin: Menard Press/New Writers' Press, 1990.

———— . *Third Person*. London: Europa Press, 1938.

———— , trans. 'Versions.' *Irish University Review* ,Vol. 5 , No. 1 (Spring 1975): 71–109.

Cohn, Robert G. *Mallarmé's Un Coup de Dés: An Exegesis*. New Haven: Yale French Studies, 1949.

———— . *Mallarmé's Masterwork: New Findings*. The Hague and Paris: Mouton, 1966.

———— . *Towards the Poems of Mallarmé*. Berkeley and Los Angeles: U of California P, 1980.

Connor, Steven. *Samuel Beckett: Repetition, Theory and Text*. Oxford: Blackwell, 1988.

Coughlan, Patricia and Davis, Alex, eds. *Modernism and Ireland: The Poetry of the 1930s*. Cork: Cork UP, 1995.

Cox, Kenneth. 'Zukofsky and Mallarmé: Notes on "A"–19'. *Maps # 5* (1973): 1–11.

Cronin, Anthony. 'The Poetry of Brian Coffey.' *The Irish Times*, 20 February 1976.

Dante Alighieri. *La Divina Commedia*, Vol. 2, *Purgatorio*. Ed. Natalino Sapegno. Firenze: Nuova Italia Editrice, 1969.

Davis, Gardner. *Vers Une Explication Rationelle du Coup de Dés*. Paris: Librairie José Corti, 1953.

Deane, Seamus, ed. *The Field Day Anthology of Irish Writing*. 3 Vols. Derry: Field Day, 1991.

Dembo, L.S. 'Interview with George Oppen.' *Contemporary Literature*, 10.2 (Spring 1969): 159–77.

Devlin, Denis. *Collected Poems*. Ed. and introd. J.C.C. Mays. Dublin: Dedalus, 1989.

Dhaenens, Jacques. *Le destin d' Orphée : 'El Desdichado' de Nerval*. Paris: Librairie Minard, 1972.

Donoghue, Denis. *We Irish: Essays on Irish Literature and Society*. Berkeley and Los Angeles: U of California P, 1986.

Eliot, T.S. *The Complete Poems and Plays*. London: Faber & Faber, 1989.

———— . 'Ulysses, Order and Myth'. In *The Dial* LXXV (Nov 1923): 480–3. Reprinted in Robert Deming ed. *James Joyce : The Critical Heritage*. 2 Vols. London : Routledge & Kegan Paul, 1970. Vol I : 268–71.

Eluard, Paul. *Oeuvres Complètes I*. Paris: Gallimard, 1968.

Ferguson, George. *Signs and Symbols in Christian Art*. New York: Oxford UP, 1954.

Ferguson, Sir Samuel. *Poems*. Dublin: Talbot Press, 1918.

Fichte, J.G. 'Some Lectures Concerning the Scholar's Vocation.' Trans. David Breazeale. In *German Idealist Philosophy*. Ed. and introd. Rüdiger Bubner. Harmondsworth : Penguin, 1997: 121–59.

Gibson, Robert. *Modern French Poets on Poetry*. Cambridge: Cambridge UP, 1961.

Hale, Terry. Review of *The Translator's Invisibility* by Lawrence Venuti. *Times Literary Supplement*, No. 4875, 6 September, 1996.

Hatlen, Burton. 'Catullus Metamorphosed.' *Paideuma*, 7.3 (Winter 1978): 539–45.

Hollander, John. *The Figure of Echo: A Mode of Allusion in Milton and After*. Berkeley and London: U of California P, 1981.

Homer. *The Iliad*. Trans. Robert Fitzgerald. Oxford: Oxford UP, 1989.

Howe, Parkman. 'Brian Coffey, An Interview.' *Eire/ Ireland*, 13.1 (Spring 1978): 113–23.

——— . 'Time and Place: The Poetry and Prose of Brian Coffey'. PhD thesis, University College Dublin, 1982.

Hrushovski, Benjamin. 'The Meaning of Sound Patterns in Poetry: An Interaction Theory.' *Poetics Today*, 2.1 (1980): 39–56.

Ince, W.N. *The Poetic Theory of Paul Valéry: Inspiration and Technique*. Leicester: Leicester UP, 1970.

Jeffreys, Mark. 'Ideologies of Lyric: A Problem of Genre in Contemporary Anglophone Poetics.' *PMLA*, 110.2 (1995): 196–205.

Joyce, James. *A Portrait of the Artist as a Young Man*. Ed. and introd. Seamus Deane. Harmondsworth: Penguin, 1992.

——— . *Ulysses*. London: Bodley Head, 1949.

Kavanagh, Patrick. *Collected Pruse*. London: MacGibbon & Kee, 1967.

Kennedy, S.B. *Irish Art and Modernism 1880–1950*. Belfast: Institute of Irish Studies, 1991.

Kenner, Hugh. *The Pound Era: The Age of Ezra Pound, T.S. Eliot, James Joyce and Wyndham Lewis*. London: Faber & Faber, 1972.

Kiberd, Declan. *Inventing Ireland*. London: Jonathan Cape, 1995.

Knowlson, James. *Damned to Fame: The Life of Samuel Beckett*. London: Bloomsbury, 1996.

La Charité, Virginia. *The Dynamics of Space : Mallarmé's Un Coup de Dés Jamais N'Abolira le Hasard*. Lexington, Kentucky: French Forum, 1987.

Lindsay, Marshall. 'Poetic Doctrine in Three of Rimbaud's Poems.' In *Rimbaud : Modern Critical Views*. Ed. Harold Bloom. New York: Chelsea House, 1988: 135–9.

Lloyd, David. *Anomalous States: Irish Writing and the Post-Colonial Movement*. Dublin: Lilliput, 1993.

Lewis, Philip E., 'The Measure of Translation Effects'. In *Difference in Translation*. Ed. Joseph Graham. Ithaca: Cornell UP, 1985 : 31–62.

MacGreevy, Thomas. *Collected Poems*. Ed. and introd. Susan Schreibman. Dublin: Anna Livia Press, 1991.

Mahon, Derek, trans. *The Chimeras*. By Gérard de Nerval. Dublin: Gallery, 1982.

——— . *Selected Poems*. London: Viking/ Gallery/ Oxford UP, 1991.

Mallarmé, Stéphane. *Mallarmé*. Trans. Anthony Hartley. Harmondsworth: Penguin , 1965.

——— . *Mallarmé: Collected Poems*. Trans. Henry Weinfield. Berkeley, Los Angeles and London: U of California P, 1994.

——— . *Oeuvres Complètes*. Ed. Henri Mondor and G. Jean-Aubry. Paris: Gallimard, 1951.

Maritain, Jacques. *Art and Scholasticism*. Trans. Joseph Evans. New York: Charles Scribner's Sons, 1962.

Mays, J.C.C. 'Brian Coffey's Work in Progress.' *Krino*, 4 (Autumn, 1987): 62–72.

––––––– . 'Passivity and Openness in Two Long Poems of Brian Coffey.' *Irish University Review*, 13.1 (Spring, 1983): 67–82.

McAllister, Andrew, ed. *The Objectivists*. Newcastle: Bloodaxe, 1996.

Miner, Earl. 'Some Issues for Study of Integrated Collections.' In *Poems in Their Place: The Intertextuality and Order of Poetic Collections*. Ed. and introd. Neil Fraistat. Chapel Hill: U of North Carolina P, 1986. 18–43.

Moore, Geoffrey, ed. *The Penguin Book of American Verse*. Harmondsworth: Penguin, 1989.

Moulin, Jeanine. *Gérard de Nerval: Les Chimères*: Geneva: Droz, 1969.

Nabokov, Vladimir. 'Problems of Translation: *Onegin* in English.' In *Theories of Translation: An Anthology of Essays from Dryden to Derrida*. Ed. Rainer Schulte and John Biguenet. Chicago and London: U of Chicago P, 1992: 127–43.

Nadal, Octave. 'Poetique et Poésie des Chimères.' *Mercure de France*, 325, (November 1955): 405–415.

Nerval, Gérard de. *Oeuvres Complètes III*. Ed. Jean Guillaume and Claude Pichois. Paris: Gallimard, 1993.

Oppen, George. *Poems of George Oppen*. Introd. Charles Tomlinson. Newcastle: Cloud, 1990.

Perloff, Marjorie. *The Dance of the Intellect: Studies on the Poetry of the Pound Tradition*. Evanston, Illinois: Northwestern UP, 1985.

Perkins, Mary Anne. *Coleridge's Philosophy : The Logos as Unifying Principle*. Oxford: Clarendon, 1994.

Preminger, Alex and Brogan, T.V.F, eds. *The New Princeton Encyclopedia of Poetry and Poetics*. Princeton, NJ: Princeton UP, 1993.

Rilke, Rainer Maria. *Selected Poetry*. Trans. Stephen Mitchell. London: Picador, 1987.

Rimbaud, Arthur. *Oeuvres Complètes*. Ed. Antoine Adam. Paris: Gallimard, 1972.

Rosenthal, M.L. and Gall, Sally M. *The Modern Poetic Sequence: The Genius of Modern Poetry*. New York and Oxford: Oxford UP, 1983.

Sealy, Douglas. Review of *Dice Thrown Never Will Annul Chance*, by Brian Coffey trans. *The Irish Times*, 24 April 1965: 10.

Silk, Michael. *Homer: The Iliad*. Cambridge: Cambridge UP, 1987.

Smith, Michael. 'Interview with Mervyn Wall about the Thirties'. *The Lace Curtain*, 4 (Summer 1971): 77–86.

Smith, Sidney B. Review of *The Chimeras* by Derek Mahon trans. *Poetry Ireland*, 7 (Spring–Summer 1983): 47–8.

Spivack, Charlotte. *George Chapman*. New York: Twayne, 1967.

Stewart, Garrett. *Reading Voices: Literature and the Phonotext*. Berkeley, Los Angeles and Oxford: U of California P, 1990.

Stierle, Karlheinz. 'Position and Negation in Mallarmé's "Prose pour des Esseintes".' Trans. Sibylle Kisro. *Yale French Studies*, 54 (1977): 96–117.

Taplin, Oliver. 'Homer.' In *Greece and the Hellenistic World*. Eds John Boardman, Jasper Griffin and Oswyn Murray. Oxford: Oxford UP, 1990: 44–71.

Venuti, Lawrence. *The Translator's Invisibility: A History of Translation*. London and NewYork: Routledge, 1995.

# INDEX